THE FIRST SWALLOWS

THE FIRST SWALLOWS

The Dawn of the Third Aliya

Leon Rubinstein

CORNWALL BOOKS
NEW YORK • TORONTO • LONDON

Cornwall Books
440 Forsgate Drive
Cranbury, N.J. 08512

Cornwall Books
25 Sicilian Avenue
London WC1A 2QH, England

Cornwall Books
2133 Royal Windsor Drive
Mississauga, Ont. L5J 1K5, Canada

Library of Congress Cataloging-in-Publication Data

Rubinstein, Leon.
  The first swallows.

  Includes index.
  1. Rubinstein, Leon. 2. Zionists—Palestine—
Biography. 3. Palestine—Emigration and immigration—
Biography. I. Title.
DS151.R73A33 1986   956.94′001′0924   83-45138
ISBN 0-8453-4758-6

Printed in the United States of America

CONTENTS

Illustrations appear as a group between pages 110 and 111.

FOREWORD

In the span of 2000 years in which the Jewish people lived in the Diaspora, they sustained the hope to return to Zion. Three times every day, the Jew prays for a renewed life in Jerusalem and Zion. At the Passover Seder, year in and year out, Jews wish each other *L'Shanah HaBa'ah B' Yerushalayim*—next year in Jerusalem. Central to the three major Jewish holidays, Passover, Shavuot and Sukkot, are themes connected with the climate of Eretz Israel. Passover, the beginning of the planting season; Shavuot, the first fruit harvest; Sukkot, the grain harvest.

These rituals served as a reminder to Jewish nationhood and helped to maintain the hope of freedom from the oppression under which the Jews lived during their long exile. During periods of catastrophe, the longing for Zion was joined with the growth of the messianic idea.

Charismatic individuals arose who took upon themselves the role of redeemer, ready to lead the Jews back to their historic homeland. These self-proclaimed messiahs attracted large numbers of supporters, people who were ready to follow them. This happened at the time of the Spanish Inquisition, a period in which Jews who would not convert to the Catholicism of the state underwent severe torture, often being subjected to the Auto-da-fe and perishing at the stake. Some of them did convert. However, secretly they retained their beliefs and rituals. They were called *Marranos*.

When the Jews were expelled from Spain in 1492, many fled to North Africa and to countries under Turkish rule—especially Eretz Israel. Among those who came there were prominent rabbis and scholars, who settled in Jerusalem, Hebron, Tiberias and Safed. Establishing yeshivot (academies), they renewed the central role which these cities played in Jewish life before they were destroyed during the Crusades. Many Jews fled to Portugal and to other European countries, notably Holland and Italy. But the Inquisition followed the Jews to Portugal, where it continued its onslaught against them.

In 1524, a mysterious traveler arrived in the Port of Venice. He said his name was David, born in Arabia in a Jewish kingdom comprising the tribes of Reuben, Gad and Manasseh. His brother was the ruler of this kingdom. David claimed to have been sent to meet with the monarchs of Europe. While the mission was secret, it was hinted that he was to gain the support of the European kings, and especially the Pope in Rome, for a war against the Turks. This Jewish tribal kingdom, with the aid of the monarchs, would wage a war to banish the Turks from the Red Sea and Eretz Israel.

David Reuveni arrived like an ambassador, riding a white horse, accompanied by an adjutant and an interpreter. After the existence of such a tribe was verified by Portuguese ship captains and consuls, he was received, personally, by Pope Clement VII. With the encouragement of the Pope, Reuveni went to Portugal in the Fall of 1525, where King Juan III promised weapons, ships, and sailors. His arrival in Portugal stirred great enthusiasm among the Marranos and raised their hopes of redemption and return to Zion. The Portuguese, however, suspected that Reuveni maintained contact with the Marranos. As a result, the support was withdrawn. He then took his mission to Venice. Again he became suspect and was banished to Spain where he was imprisoned. After a few years he died there. Thus a period of hope ended in disappointment and depression.

A century later, the Ukrainian general Bogdan Chmelnitsky led a successful peasant revolt against the Polish nobility. His armies overran towns and villages, ravaging hundreds of Jewish communities and massacring Jews as they went. This tragedy had a depressing effect on the Jews of Europe, creating an atmosphere of defeat throughout the communities.

In the summer of 1665, a man arose who would claim to be the deliverer of the Jewish people. Sabbatai Zevi, born in the city of Smyrna in Asia Minor, visited Jerusalem. He proclaimed himself the messiah who would deliver his people, the Jews, from the Diaspora and lead them to Eretz Israel. To spread the message of Sabbatai's "godly" mission, Nathan Ashkenazi of Gaza, his trusted supporter, sent the following message to the dispersed Jewish communities:

> Be informed that our Messiah was born in Smyrna and is called Sabbatai Zevi. Soon he will reveal his kingdom to the world, will wrest the crown from the King of Ishmael (Sultan of Turkey) and place it on his own head.

This announcement created an upheaval among the Jewish masses. Whole communities expressed their readiness to follow him. In Smyrna, on Rosh HaShanah, his appearance at the synagogue brought cries of "Long live our king, our messiah."

This messianic movement grew significantly, influencing Sabbatai to transfer his activities to Constantinople. However, when his entourage reached its destination, Sabbatai was arrested by the Turkish police and imprisoned. Groups of believers, hearing of his incarceration, came to the prison to visit their Messiah. To isolate Sabbatai from his supporters, he was transferred to Gallipoli where he was placed under guard in a castle tower for pretending to the crown.

In response to the growth of the Sabbatean movement, Sultan Mahmud IV ordered Sabbatai Zevi to appear in his residence in Adrianople, where in September, 1666, he was given the option to convert to Islam or to suffer execution as a traitor. Sabbatai placed the Turkish turban on his head, thus declaring his readiness to convert to Islam. The "new Muslim" assumed the name of Mahmed Effendi and was given the title "protector of the Sultan's palace."

Remarkably, Sabbatai's followers continued to believe in this false Messiah, refusing to allow their faith to be shaken. To the majority of the Jews, however, this episode brought depression, disappointment and hopelessness.

It is commonly held that the suffering and persecution which the "wandering Jews" underwent were the forces that held the Jewish people together. This is only one side of the coin. In the many years of the Diaspora, both in good times like the Golden Epoch in Spain and during periods of intolerance and persecution, the cultural activities within the Jewish communities continued uninterrupted. Important personalities worked in a variety of fields—poetry, literature, philosophy, and Talmudic studies—affecting the entire Jewish world.

Rabbi Shlomo Yitzhaki (Rashi) lived in the Lorraine Province of southern France during the eleventh century; his work was widely recognized by Jewish scholars. A vintner, Rashi devoted his free time to writing commentaries and interpretations of the Talmud and the Bible. The Commentaries on the Five Books of Moses, written in simple language, were immediately accepted as authoritative. To this day, children start their biblical studies using "Chumash with Rashi" as the standard text.

In the twelfth century, the Rambam (Rabbi Moses Maimonides) wrote his great works, *Mishneh Torah* and *More Nevuhim (Guide to the Perplexed)*. These works rationalized Talmudic law and Jewish thought. Maimonides, through these works, influenced the direction of Jewish law and philosophy for centuries.

The most influential scholar of the sixteenth century was Joseph Caro. Born in Spain, Caro fled to Asia Minor as a child with his parents, later settling in Safed in Eretz Israel. For decades, he devoted himself to the writing of a codex of rabbinical law which became the primary "law book" for the *Beth Din* in Jewish life. This four-volume masterwork embraced every legal aspect of Jewish life from worship to Sabbath and Holiday observances, life-cycle events, marriage and divorce, and court practice. He later condensed and simplified his work into the *Shulchan Aruch* (the Set Table), which became the standard codex of Jewish law used until the present in *Beth Din* (Rabbinical Court). A further condensation, the *Kitzur Shulchan Aruch,* is used as a source for laymen to answer basic questions of daily life. These two texts acted as a strong unifying force through the centuries and remain so now.

In the eighteenth century, as the liberal winds of change emanated from France and Germany, Jews remained without civil rights. In Germany, during this period, Moses the son of Mendel (Mendelssohn) from Dessau, began to study the German language and literature and some of the newly-developed sciences. Mendelssohn was a student of Jacob Frankel, the rabbi of Dessau, who later was invited to assume the position of rabbi of Berlin. Mendelssohn decided to follow Rabbi Frankel, and after great difficulty received permission to enter Berlin. Once there, he began writing essays on metaphysics and literature, in German, soon becoming known among the German intelligensia. In a contest sponsored by the Prussian Academy of Science his essay won first prize. Parenthetically, the eminent philosopher Immanuel Kant, a participant in the contest, received only an honorable mention.

Mendelssohn's accomplishments attracted the famous writer and philosopher Gotthold Lessing. The relationship became close; Lessing later used Mendelssohn as the model for the central character in his novel *Nathan the Wise*. Mendelssohn's philosophical works, especially *Fedon* and *Jerusalem,* earned him the name of the "Jewish Socrates." Recognized by the German emperor Friedrich the Great, he was granted permanent residence and privileges in the Prussian capital, Berlin. Mendelssohn believed that as Jews learned the German language and literature, they could be taken from their cultural isolation and brought nearer to German society. He translated the Bible into a modern literary German in Hebrew script, using it as an educational device for learning German.

Mendelssohn's successful attempts to integrate the Jews into German society, however, were directed at the individual Jew, not the Jewish people as a nation. This direction, in both Germany and France, created a new problem: assimilation. Many Jews in these countries, including Mendelssohn's own children, began to assimilate. Some later converted to Christianity.

While the clarion call of the French Revolution was *"liberte, egalite, fraternite,"* Jews were not accorded civil rights until three years after the Declaration of the Rights of Man. In 1804 Napoleon Bonaparte was proclaimed emperor. In 1807 he convened a Sanhedrin of rabbis and laymen at which he forced upon the Jewish community a declaration denying the nationhood of the Jews. In exchange for citizenship, the Jews abandoned their peoplehood and became individual citizens of the French empire of "Mosaic persuasion." The result was a movement toward assimilation and, in some cases, conversion to Christianity.

Jews in Western Europe became attracted to the cultural and intellectual currents of the period. Some became leading advocates of universal political ideas, such as Karl

Marx and Ferdinand LaSalle. Jews became prominent in music, the arts and sciences, innovators and leaders in their respective fields. However, they did not devote their creative energies toward the Jewish issues of the day. The major work of Jewish scholarship in the second half of the nineteenth century was in Biblical criticism, an historical approach which negated the vitality of contemporary Judaism.

A new phenomenon did occur in Western Europe as a result of the Emancipation. Reform Judaism emerged in 1818 with the founding of the first Reform synagogue. It was a revolt against traditional forms of worship, a repudiation of the rabbinical structure and the messianic concept of the return. Instead, the idea of "Israel's mission," focussing in the Diaspora, was formulated. Its foremost advocates, Samuel Holdheim and Abraham Geiger, severed Judaism from its national roots. The Reform movement, which originated in Germany, spread into other countries. A more extreme movement, Liberal Judaism, was organized in London in 1836. German Jews brought this new idea with them to America. Most notable among the reformers in the United States was Isaac Mayer Wise who institutionalized Reform Judaism in this country.

In reaction to the spread of reform, a variety of new formulations emerged within the traditionalist community. Samson Raphael Hirsch, rabbi of Frankfurt, developed a strict traditional philosophy, accommodating the trappings of modernity but not altering the basis liturgical structure.

In 1840, the world was shocked by a "blood libel" against the Jews of Damascus. On February 5 of that year, Father Thomas, the head of the Franciscan monastery, disappeared with his servant. Soon after, a poor Jewish barber, after being tortured, "confessed" that the men were murdered for ritual purposes. Tension heightened; several Jewish leaders were arrested for complicity in this act.

When the news reached Europe and the United States, mass meetings were held, protesting the blood libel. These meetings were attended by both Christians and Jews. Sir Moses Montefiore, the Sheriff of London, and the prominent French lawyer, Adolphe Cremieux, proceeded to Alexandria and secured orders from the Egyptian governor, Mahmet Ali, for the release of the Jewish leaders. They were received in Constantinople by the Sultan of Turkey, who unconditionally acquitted the Jews, pronouncing the accusation of ritual murder a gross libel.

The pressures of assimilation and anti-Semitism produced often conflicting reactions in Jewish life. The Jews of Western Europe, especially, were confronted with the antithetical forces of tradition vs. modernity, religion vs. secularism, national identity vs. emancipation.

Moses Hess, who was raised in a religious home in Bonn, Germany, discarded Jewish tradition in his early youth. He embraced, instead, the philosophies of Spinoza and Hegel and became active in the revolutionary movements of his time. Intimate in circles of Marx and Engels, he became a leader of the internationalist, socialist movements following the abortive German Revolution in 1848.

Shocked by the trauma of the Damascus Blood Libel and influenced by the philosophy of the contemporaneous Italian national liberation movement, Hess moved toward a Jewish nationalist approach. His latent feelings of peoplehood brought him to understand that the Jews must, as a nation, fight for their liberation simultaneously with the community of other nations.

In 1862, he published *Rome and Jerusalem,* which signalled his return to his people. An interesting and important treatise, the book synthesizes the internationalism of the revolutionary movements with the particularism of Jewish peoplehood.

Hess refutes the idea that assimilation is an end in itself. It will not solve the Jewish problem. He suggests that the reconstitution, in Palestine, of a viable Jewish community, is the real solution.

Jews are a people whose history runs parallel to the history of other peoples. Now, when the historical process brings these peoples to rejuvenate, our nation has also to be redeemed. As long as a Jew will deny his nationhood, he will not show his solidarity with his persecuted people. His personal situation will become intolerable.

Hess continues: "Put on thousands of masks. Change your name. Change your religion and customs to hide your origins. It will not help you."

Hess turned to the millions of Jews of Russia and Poland who still harbored the desire to be redeemed and urged them to organize a movement to emigrate to Palestine to revive a national life in the Biblical homeland. Only after two decades did his ideas gain attention. With the rise of a reactionary government in Russia, Jewish leaders altered their attitudes and realized the value of his proposed solution to the Jewish Problem.

Until 1881, many Russian schools had been open to Jewish students, and Jews were accorded some economic and social standing. As a result, numbers of Jews had embraced "Mother Russia" with patriotic enthusiasm. The *Haskalah* reached Russian Jewry, but it took a different direction than it had in Germany. In Russia, several literary works appeared in Hebrew expressing the longing for "return to Zion." These novels and poems influenced the growth of Jewish nationalism in Russia. Most influential among these writers were Peretz Smolenskin, Abraham Mapu, Moses Lilienblum and the poet, Juda Leib Gordon. They depicted the glories of ancient Judea and encouraged the Jews to return to the land where a proud Jewish people had once lived.

On March 13, 1881, Czar Alexander II was assassinated. This act signalled the end of Jewish civil rights in Russia. Two months later, the infamous May Laws were enacted, expelling Jews from the villages and towns and restricting them in their trades and professions. Jews began to emigrate in large numbers, going to the free countries in Western Europe and, primarily, to the Americas—the United States, Canada, and Argentina.

As a reaction to the May Laws and pogroms in southern Russia, a group of students organized themselves to take a radical step toward auto-emancipation, to become pioneers in Palestine. They called themselves BILU, an acronym for the biblical phrase "House of Jacob, Let Us Go." The first group of 14 reached the port of Jaffa in July, 1882. They, and others who followed, looked for work at the wineries of Baron Edmund de Rothschild in Rishon LeZion and Zichron Yaacov and at the Mikveh Israel Agricultural School, founded several years before by the French society, Alliance Israelite Universelle. The wineries were administered under autocratic rule by representatives of the Baron. Unsatisfied with this situation and impelled by their idealism, some of the Biluim organized the first BILU colony, Gedera. A second colony, Haderah, was organized around the same time in Samaria by Jerusalem Jews.

Not having previous experience in agriculture, not being able to adjust to the climate of Palestine, and suffering from malaria, some of the young settlers returned, disappointed, to Europe. Those who remained began to employ local Arab workers. The pioneering spirit which they had brought with them to Palestine waned.

In 1903, a pogrom was perpetrated in the Bessarabian city of Kishinev. Jews were slaughtered, their homes plundered. Pogroms spread to other Jewish communities. Chaim Nachman Bialik, the Hebrew poet, in reaction to the pogroms, forcefully reprimanded the Jews in his poems "Al HaShchita" and "Ir Ha-Harega," for not fighting back while their kin were being tortured and murdered. Instead, they hid in order to save themselves. Many young Jews, horrified by the pogroms and disappointed in the lack of response by the revolutionary movements, organized defense groups. The first such group was founded by the Poale Zion in the city of Homel.

That same year, Dr. Theodore Herzl brought a proposal from Great Britain to the World Zionist Congress for Jewish colonization of Uganda. Since the Turkish government had refused a charter for Jewish colonization in Palestine, he recommended the acceptance of this plan as a temporary measure for the relief of the persecuted Jews of Russia. The Congress was severely divided. While many delegates supported the Uganda Project, the Russian Zionists, led by Menachem Ussishkin and Dr. Yehiel Tshlenoff, rejected it out of hand.

The two shocking events—the Kishinev pogrom and the Uganda proposal—stirred many young Zionists to re-evaluate their personal outlooks. Many of them decided to immigrate to Palestine, leaving their homes to live a new productive life on the soil of Eretz Israel.

Early in 1904, individual Jews began to arrive at the port of Jaffa—men and women who were determined to lead an entirely different life than they had in the towns and villages in their native Poland, Lithuania, the Ukraine, and Romania. Yeshiva students, tradespeople, mechanics and gymnasium students, they were not satisfied with a Zionism of speeches, selling *shkolim* and *Keren Kayemet* stamps. They came, at first, singly. Soon hundreds followed.

It was an aliyah that based itself on the principles of self-realization, self-labor, no exploitation of workers, and equality of the sexes. Revival of Hebrew as the spoken language was a primary goal. For the newcomers to carry out these principles meant radically altering their life style and undergoing extraordinary hardships. They were unaccustomed to the climate. Unemployment was widespread; often they went without food. Many of the young people succumbed to illness, especially malaria. The newcomers, too, suffered from an unfriendly atmosphere in the existing Jewish colonies when they sought work. Claiming that these young people were too weak to do manual labor, the colonists refused to hire them. Many, frustrated and discouraged, could not endure and left the country.

Determined to overcome the antipathy of the landowners, those who stayed started to compete with the experienced Arab workers in the olive orchards and orange groves. With persistence, they matched the speed of the Arab workers as they softened the soil with their hoes, ignoring the pain of swollen, blistered hands. They called this *Kibbush Avodah,* the conquest of labor! As their hands calloused, so did their character take shape. As a result of their perseverence, many landowners engaged them as permanent workers. Those who remained were steeled by their trials, gaining strength of both body and character. They became the paradigms for the future generations.

The members of this aliyah, in fact, became the creators and leaders of the Jewish state in the making. These men and women inspired and influenced the pioneers and the Zionists dispersed throughout the world, not with oratory, but with their deeds. Outstanding among them was Aaron David Gordon, who came to Eretz Israel in 1904 at the age of 48. In Russia, he had never done manual labor. Two other men who would become prominent in the process of the Second Aliyah arrived in Jaffa at the same time as Gordon. Eliezer and Israel Shochat, two brothers, set out to seek work in Petach Tikvah.

Gordon and Eliezer Shochat had common characteristics. Each was a deep thinker who spoke softly, sparingly and precisely. Not satisfied with working only in the citrus groves, Shochat moved to the Galilee, where he was able to plow his own land and grow wheat and corn. He was joined there by his friend Shlomo Zemach. Together, they organized *Ha Horesh,* the plowman's organization. Eliezer's younger brother, Israel, followed them to the Galilee.

During this period, agricultural colonies were endangered by marauders from the neighboring Arab villages. To protect the colonies, *Hashomer,* the Watchman, was organized by former members of the Homel self-defense organization led by Israel Shochat. It was a dangerous undertaking, for the Arab guards, who had been employed by the colonists, vigorously opposed the formation of a Jewish cadre of watchmen. After repelling several attacks by the Arab guards, the *Shomrim* firmly established themselves in the colonies. *HaRoeh*—the shepherd—followed. This group undertook to guard the grazing flocks of sheep in the pastures against attack during the night.

A significant impetus to the success of the Second Aliyah in the agricultural development of the country was the implementation of a policy made by the World Zionist Organization to embark on a program of practical colonization in Palestine. In April, 1908, the Palestine Bureau was established in Jaffa with Dr. Arthur Ruppin at its head. The Bureau organized the Palestine Land Development Company. Its first task was the growing of olive saplings on Jewish National Fund land for the planting of a Herzl Forest in Ben Shemen and Hulda.

At the same time, a training farm was established in Daleika (Kinneret) on the shores of the Sea of Galilee, headed by the agronomist B. Berman. A conflict arose between Berman and the workers. Some of the men and women left the farm and went to Hadera to train there; others insisted on his removal. To settle the dispute, Dr. Ruppin decided to divide the farm in two. On the east side of the lake, in an area called Um Juni, land was given to the splinter group to work on its own. When the experiment proved successful, Dr. Ruppin invited the experienced workers from Hadera to take over the land permanently. Thus, the first *kvutzah*—renamed *Degania* (cornflower)—was founded in December, 1910.

Having no model to emulate, the members of Degania had to create their own pattern for communal living. In the evenings they would gather in the dining room to discuss the problems that had arisen and plan the next day's work in the fields and orchards. They discussed how to achieve the goal of creating a society based on social justice, self-labor and the conquest of the soil. They struggled with the problems of managing a collective economy, the role of women in the work structure and the rearing of children. The members become a tightly-knit family, sharing their ideas, their experience and their responsibilities. Life was difficult. They lived in tents and slept on floors. Many of the members fell ill. Yet, they continued their enterprise without letup. Gradually, they expanded and diversified their work into new areas in order to increase their yield.

The Kinneret farm became a commune in 1912. 20 dunams of land were set aside to establish an agricultural training school for girls, organized by Chana Meisel.

By 1914, before the First World War, the conference of agricultural workers was able to report that there were approximately 4000 men and women engaged in agricultural work.

Because of the outbreak of the war, the Turkish government ordered the deportation of citizens of the allied countries from Palestine, particularly Russian citizens. Among them were David Ben-Gurion and Itzhak Ben-Zvi. Soon, General Gamal Pasha, the Turkish governor, began confiscating Jewish property. In 1915, he issued an order forbidding the distribution and use of JNF stamps, the flying of the Zionist flag and the use of the Magen David emblem.

During this period of oppression, a new leadership arose

to alleviate the suffering of the population. This leadership created the institutions that would not only solve short-term problems, but would develop as important institutions for the future. At the initiation of Berl Katznelson, Shlomo Levi, and M. Rutberg of Kinneret, *Ha Mashbir* was organized to provide food for workers in Judea at reduced prices. Abraham Harzfeld assumed the task of finding jobs for needy workers. He proposed that workers contribute five percent of their earnings to a loan fund for the unemployed. To provide both jobs and essential services, Harzfeld established a cooperative bakery and a laundry. Thus, he inspired hope and confidence.

Turkish oppression continued. In 1917, the regime expelled 9,000 Jews from Jerusalem, Tel Aviv and the surrounding areas. Jews were beaten on the streets indiscriminately by army patrols, and arrested. About 120 people were taken, on foot, to Damascus on suspicion of spying. Many of them died of hunger and disease.

Harzfeld mobilized the delivery of food and medicine to the prisoners. Carrying a false Austrian passport, and with the help of bribery, he reached a high Turkish official, winning the right to visit the prisoners. He encouraged them, promising that he would do whatever possible to gain their release. Immediately after the British army liberated Damascus, Harzfeld appealed to them to transport the Jewish prisoners in the Turkish jails to Palestine. The military commander hesitated. Thereupon, Harzfeld organized the prisoners and led them, on foot, back to Palestine.

With the arrival of the halutzim of the Third Aliyah, Harzfeld became instrumental in purchasing land for JNF to begin the colonization of the Emek. When the Histadrut was organized, he became secretary of its colonization department. In this position, he initiated the *homah u'migdal*—stockade and tower—settlements in the 1930's. In response to the restrictions by the Mandatory Power against the construction of new settlements, he took advantage of a still-existing Turkish law prohibiting the removal of buildings with roofs. Harzfeld organized hundreds of people from neighboring kibbutzim who, in the dark of night, placed prefabricated huts in the hills, thus creating a new reality.

The past three aliyot were halutzic ones. The BILU of 1882 heralded the real dawn of the realization of modern zionism. The Second Aliyah, which started in 1904, laid the foundations of the state-in-the-making—populating the land, modernizing the Hebrew language and establishing economic realities. When the young pioneers arrived in Palestine, they found a neglected, desolate, arid landscape, almost without vegetation. Determined to create new realities, they transformed the land and the society.

After the First World War, the Third Aliyah started to arrive. Building upon the foundation created by its predecessors, the members of the Third Aliyah expanded the settlement process and institutionalized the cooperative ventures. The young people, writers, poets, and students formed a *gdud avodah*—a work battalion. They hewed stones, paved roads and erected buildings. As greater numbers arrived from the *hachsharah* (training) farms, the small kvutzot expanded, and kibbutzim of 1,000 or more members were created. The first large kibbutz, Ein Harod, was established in the Emek. The kibbutzim undertook to diversify their agriculture and introduced the raising of livestock and poultry. The kibbutz became a major institution in the Yishuv. At the same time, the first *Moshav* (cooperative farm)—Nahalal—was organized in the Emek. From the roots of HaShomer grew the Haganah, an expanded defense organization. The Histadrut, the united labor federation, founded in December, 1920, provided health care and educational and training services. It created, as well, major worker-owned industries, many of which were consolidated into Koor Industries in 1944.

The Third Aliyah brought with it new leaders, notably Chaim Arlasoroff, Golda Meir and Eliezer Kaplan, who made tremendous contributions in bringing Israel to statehood. When the quasi-governmental body, the Va'ad Leumi, was organized, its leadership consisted mainly of the members of the Second and Third Aliyot. Even after the middle-class immigrants of the Fourth and Fifth Aliyot were settled, the leadership of the yishuv remained in the hands of the original pioneers. It was only natural, therefore, that these people would remain at the helm when the State of Israel was proclaimed in 1948, a role which they played for the next three decades.

In 1982, one hundred years of Zionist colonization was celebrated. The dominant circles of the current Likud government of Israel used this occasion to attempt to rewrite history for the purpose of self-aggrandizement and political reasons. They minimized the role of the labor pioneers—the halutzim—going so far as to belittle the role of Israel's first prime minister, David Ben-Gurion, in order to inflate the accomplishments of their own party and its leaders. The revisionists who now attempt to grab credit originally did not participate in preparing the institutions of the state-on-its-way. They believed that Jewish youth should be educated solely towards a political solution. They organized a paramilitary youth movement in Poland, emphasizing uniforms, riflery and parading, pretending that this was the manner to fight for the establishment of the Jewish State.

Chaim Weizmann, Israel's first president, commenting on the necessity to create the institutions and infrastructure of a society said "You don't get a state on a silver platter."

The following memoirs give a portrait of the ardent halutzim who adhered to the constructive way of life while prepared to make every sacrifice, of sweat and blood, to create, develop and preserve a free democratic State of Israel.

PREFACE

THIS BOOK OF MEMOIRS was written as I approached my 80th birthday. It consists of two parts—my early days as a child in Poland, surrounded by a large family steeped in Jewish tradition; and my youth as a *Halutz* in the land of Israel, to which I ascended shortly after the close of the first World War. The account of my fourteen months in Israel—a sojourn that ended all too quickly because of serious illness—is based on a diary which I kept, and on vivid memories of that exciting period in my life and in the life of the renascent Jewish homeland. I have included a detailed account of the trek from Poland to Eretz Israel which I made with a group of comrades across the highways and byways of Poland, Austria, Yugoslavia, Italy, and Egypt, until we at last crossed the border of Eretz Israel. The ordeal of reaching the Promised Land was often no less difficult than the process of taking root in the long-neglected soil.

I am deeply grateful to Abraham Shulman, who edited the original Yiddish manuscript, which was published serially in the *Jewish Daily Forward*. Mr. Shulman integrated into the story some of my writings on the Second *Aliya* which I had prepared as background to the *Halutzic* epoch which laid the foundation for the future Jewish State, as well as sketches of outstanding personalities who exercised great influence in that period, the decade before World War I.

I wish to acknowledge the role of Avinoam Korn, a former emissary from Israel to the Youth and Education Department of the Jewish National Fund in America, who chanced to hear about my diary during a chat with me, a diary which I had in my possession for over fifty years. He inspired me to make it public.

A special thanks to Shoshanna Koven, my former secretary, who with true devotion typed up my dictated Yiddish manuscript.

This English version is the work of my Labor Zionist colleague, Nahum Guttman, who translated from the Yiddish not only the language but the spirit of my book.

Leon Rubinstein

THE FIRST SWALLOWS

MY FAMILY

I WAS BORN ON FEBRUARY 2, 1901, IN THE POLISH CITY OF Lodz. My father's family—my grandfather and great-grand-father—were in the textile industry in Zgierz, but my father Leizer (Eliezer) moved to Lodz when he married my mother, Baltscha, whose family was also in the textile business. As fate would have it, my father was in America on business when the first World War broke out, so my mother took her brood—my four brothers, my sister and myself—to live in the home that my father inherited in Zgierz. I was then of *bar mitzva* age.

I remained in Zgierz until I went on Aliya to Eretz Israel in December 1918.

As in most Jewish towns throughout Poland, there was in Zgierz a lively community, complete with *chedorim* and a *Yeshiva*, as well as secular schools. Zgierz also had many Jewish cultural organizations and personalities, a large library named after David Frischman; the sculptor Mark Schwartz, son of the distinguished (Maskil) Issachar Schwartz; the Hebrew poets Yakov Kahan, Yitzhak Katznelson and others. The Yiddish writer Yehuda Elberg, who now lives in Montreal, also hails from Zgierz.

The Jews of Zgierz earned their livelihood in many ways, but the major source of sustenance was the textile industry, with its rhythm of spinning wheels and weaving machines. Zgierz had a number of large factories which employed their own workers. There were also smaller textile plants which

29

farmed out their jobs to contractors, home-workers, shearers and fabric makers. When mechanical weaving machines were introduced, the Zgierz weavers adapted themselves to the modern techniques. A considerable number of people were engaged in the textile industry. The factory owners were Germans and Jews while the workers were Jews, Germans and Poles. Some factories sent out their own salesmen deep into Russia while some worked in tandem with industries in nearby Lodz. In other words, Zgierz lived by the rhythm of the weaving industry, and in this rhythm my family also lived—my father, grandfather and great-grandfather.

My father, Eliezer Rubinstein, was a third-generation textile manufacturer. Back in the middle of the nineteenth century my great-grandfather had a weaving plant in Zgierz. In those days, only German masterweavers could be employed, because they belonged to guilds which excluded all others. My aunt Yachtsha, my father's older sister, loved to tell us little children stories about our grandfather Joseph, who died when I was eighteen months old. Aunt Yachtsha lived with her mother, our grandmother Malkele Rubinstein, and whenever we came to visit, Aunt Yachtsha told us stories about Grandfather Joseph.

One of those stories became deeply etched in my memory. Once, when grandfather came home from the *beth hamidrash*, his father was stomping around the room in a nervous state. When asked what the matter was, great-grandfather replied that he had had a sharp exchange with his German masterweaver, who called him a "verfluchter Yude," whereupon great-grandfather threw out the offensive German. The German turned around and sarcastically declared that Rubinstein would yet have to beg him to come back to work.

When grandfather Joseph heard this, he tried to calm his father, saying, "You won't have to do that because I'll run the factory."

This was an unexpected remark, and great-grandfather looked at him with astonishment. It never occurred to him that his son Joseph, this perpetual student at the *beth hamidrash*, had any interest in the factory. My grandfather then revealed that for a long time, whenever he came home from *beth hamidrash*, he would drop in at the factory and ask the masterweaver how the machinery functioned. He was interested in every detail of production. The master, impressed by his zeal and sincere curiosity, explained everything.

My grandfather demonstrated that he could manage the factory, and that's how it was.

Grandfather Joseph later taught the skills to members of his own family. He also accepted students from nearby towns. Understandably, among his apprentices were his own sons and sons-in-law, and even the daughters. Eventually my grandfather played an important role in the textile industry, not only in Zgierz but in the entire region.

After the second World War, a memorial volume, *Sefer Zgierz*, was published in Israel to commemorate the martyrs of the town. Some of the contributors told about my grandfather's pioneering role. Leon Lifshitz, in his memoir, "My Hometown at the End of the 19th Century," relates: "The Jewish textile industry in Zgierz began with Reb Yossel Rubinstein, a pious Jew of great ability, who was the first to learn the weaving trade and developed generations of weavers and weavermasters, who founded factories in Zgierz, Lodz and in the surrounding towns. . ."

Another contributor, I. L. Weinstein, wrote that the Zgierz clothmakers ". . .felt the influence of Yossel Rubinstein. He trained a generation of skilled weavers and masterweavers. Out of his factory came well-known Zgierz and Lodz clothmakers."

More particulars about my grandfather were presented by Dr. Abraham Eiger in an article about his own father, Moishel Eiger, who was one of the richest manufacturers in Zgierz

31

and an important figure in the town's Jewish cultural life. Dr. Eiger wrote:

His life, and especially the younger years of my father, were intertwined with the life of his uncle Reb Yossel Rubinstein. After Moishel's father died during the cholera epidemic, his education was in the hands of his mother, Zisele, and her brother, Yossel Rubinstein. . . . Yossel Rubinstein was the first in Zgierz to set up manual workshops. He quickly mastered the German language and studied the basics of the industry from the technical literature. He established contacts with Jewish manufacturers in the Sudetenland and became known as a textile specialist. Students came to him not only from neighboring Lodz, Ozerkow and other towns, but also from Lithuania, Podolia, and so on. . . .

This was the first Jewish textile school in the area. Rubinstein accepted students for a two-year course, including room and board which his wife Malkele tended to. Among his students were his sons Meir and Leizer, and his sons-in-law Abraham Zilberschatz and Leizer Shtachelberg, as well as Moishel Eiger. . . . Having a diploma from Rubinstein, Moishel Eiger was hired as weavermaster by one of the largest Jewish firms in Lodz, owned by Moshe Aaron Wiener.

So much for my father's side. My mother, Baltscha, was born in Lodz. Her family was associated with the textile industry and commerce. My great-grandfather on my mother's side, Mordecai Shmuel Lipschitz, was one of the first Jewish residents in Lodz, the great textile center of Poland and indeed of all Russia. Once Lodz was only a small village called Wilki, so named because of the wolves abounding in the nearby forests. My great-grandfather was a wealthy landowner. He sold land to German immigrants who developed the new textile industry in the growing urban center.

My great-grandfather gave his sons a traditional religious education. The eldest son, Rabbi Alexander Ziskind Lipschitz, became rabbi of Ozerkow and was renowned in the entire region. As in many Jewish families of the time, sons received a thorough religious education while daughters were given secular studies. My grandmother, Golda Miriam, the oldest daughter, actually got private tutoring, which included general subjects and languages: Russian, Polish and German. She married Aaron Rosenblum, who was born in Klein-Biali.

After the wedding, they settled in Lodz, where he dealt in yarn. My grandmother and grandfather were of two different worlds. He was extremely pious and a fanatic *Gerer Hassid*, while she, though an observant woman, was what today would be called "progressive." Nonetheless, their family life was idyllic. My grandfather held her in high esteem and she, with her many capabilities, helped him immensely in his business affairs.

My grandmother loved to read. It is interesting to note that while they had gas and electric lights in the house, she would read at night by candle, the candlestick standing on a marble-topped table. She read until it flickered out.

When I was ten years old, my grandmother sent me to the library to fetch her some books. When I informed the librarian that the books were for my grandmother, she said, "Oh, yes, for Madam Rosenblum I have set aside some new books which have just arrived. She has been a constant reader here for decades."

As to their own children, my grandparents kept the same tradition: sons received an intensive religious training and daughters attended the *gymnasium*.

Among my earliest recollections, I recall my great-grandfather on my mother's side, who had a two-story house in the center of Lodz, at the corner of Pieterkovska and Tzegelnyana. My great-grandmother was already dead, and he lived with his youngest daughter, Zippora Glovinsky, a young widow with five children.

On the first floor of the huge house was a spacious salon. My great-grandfather did not allow his children to talk him into breaking up this salon into smaller rooms. He wanted to keep it intact, because each year he gathered the whole tribe for a Purim feast. Those Purim festivals, during his lifetime, and continued after his death by his eldest daughter, Golda Miriam, were among the most colorful moments of my childhood.

We all came to the Purim feast—all the descendents of my great-grandfather: children, grandchildren and great-grandchildren. He was in his eighties and walked with a cane. Because of his weak eyesight, and because there were so many of us, he did not always recognize his offspring, and could not tell one from another. I remember approaching him once, as he leaned on my cousin Michael Glovinsky. He asked who I was and cousin Michael replied: "He is Baltsha-Golda-Miriam's." I was upset that my own great-grandfather did not recognize me.

Great-grandfather himself conducted the Purim festivities. He sat at the head of the table like a king enthroned. Around the table sat all the children, according to age, male and female. Then came the grandchildren, and finally the tiny tots of the next generation. At his side were two bowls, one with silver coins and one with copper. Dressed in our finest clothes, we ate heartily of the appetizing goodies—the *haman-taschen*—and waited impatiently for the climax of the party, the *Purimspielers*. Then the doors opened and with great fanfare the masked players trooped in to present their Purim variety show, including "The Selling of Joseph."

Great-grandfather would later hand the actors coins according to his estimate of whether the actors were very poor people—they would get silver coins—or ordinary *shnorers*, who would get coppers.

Of course, we children also got Purim gifts.

After my great-grandfather passed away, the Purim holiday was celebrated at my maternal grandparents home. There, we children sometimes staged our own *Purimspiel*.

Grandfather was well off, and also a good and friendly

man, but he was nicknamed "the miser." That was because of his habit of shaking his head and saying "no" whenever a relative in need came for some help. He insisted that "money is a great thing" and one should be careful with it. But after taking a close look at the supplicant relative, his heart would soften and he would be forthcoming and generous.

Because of this characteristic, I decided to teach grandfather a lesson. I organized the grandchildren to pose as "police" during one Purim feast. We dressed up as policemen in makeshift uniforms and loudly proclaimed that if grandfather didn't give us each a whole ruble, we would sequester the furniture. We each had gummed paper in our hands and threatened that if our demands were not met we would paste the paper on the mirrors. Grandfather was shaken by this threat, as he was an extraordinarily neat person. The salon floor was of a fine inlaid wood. Every item of furniture was polished and the mirrors shone brilliantly. To paste gummed paper on those mirrors would be vandalism of the worst sort. Grandfather turned white and paid us the ransom money— the stipulated ruble apiece. But he did not forget to rib us: "What will you do with so much money?"

As for my education, I was sent to a *cheder* where classes were limited to eighteen pupils at most. My classmates were scions of wealthy *Hassidic* families. My Talmud teacher, Joseph Alexanderer, was a tall, large-boned Jew with an attractive beard. His merit was not that he was such a great scholar but that he was a disciplinarian, and from time to time he would belay his charges with a mean slap in the face.

As was customary, we began a new lesson on Sunday, and reviewed it on Monday, Tuesday and Wednesday. On Thursday we were examined. I had a sharp mind, and by Tuesday I knew the lesson by heart. On Wednesday I would look into the *Gemorrah* out of boredom. In the middle of the lesson, I would play games and horse around with my classmates with my hands under the table.

Once the rabbi noticed that I was not looking into the *Ge-*

morrah and he suddenly sprang a question on me. Calmly, I answered correctly. This disappointed him—that I was able to reply correctly without concentrating on the textbook. He reprimanded me loudly: "*Sheigetz*—you are smart but you don't want to study! You have answered like the 'Maharsha'" (a famous Talmudic commentator of the seventeenth century). He gave me a hefty slap on the cheek. Normally, when the rabbi slapped me I kept quiet, but this time I broke out in tears—he hit me because I *knew* my lesson! I ran home and told my father that I didn't want to study with this rabbi anymore. And I didn't.

My father enrolled me in a modern *cheder* where I had two teachers. One was a Litvak named Kamenietsky, and the other, a Pole, a Rabbi Rosenberg. Kamenietsky was a *baal dikduk*, a scholarly grammarian. With him I studied the Bible and Hebrew grammar. Rosenberg taught us Hebrew language and literature and Jewish history. He was beloved by his pupils because of his heartiness and he exercised great influence over us. Rosenberg was a wonderful educator and he related countless legends of the Talmud. Every holiday eve he would tell us tales of great Jewish personalities and heroes which kindled our fantasies.

I remember the story, "Arrow of Salvation," of the Bar Kochba era, about a Jewish lad whose father fought against the Romans. When there was a shortage of weapons, the boy fashioned an arrow out of his toys and found his way to the battlefield. He reached his father just as the last arrow had been spent. The father took his son's arrow and aimed it at the head of the Roman commander, who fell dead. The Roman soldiers fled in panic and the Jews celebrated a great victory because of this little boy's valor. In later years, on *Lag B'Omer*, I would tell this story to my own pupils, who enjoyed it immensely.

My father bought me many small Hebrew storybooks, which were put out by various publishers. He also subscribed to *Ben Hashachar* and other children's magazines. I was a passionate reader and devoured everything in Hebrew. I read *Memories of the House of David*, Kalman Shulman's history of the world, and Hebrew poetry as well as George Eliot's *Daniel Deronda* which had been translated into Hebrew by David Frischman. In the modern *cheder* we also read the poems of Chaim Nachman Bialik, Y. L. Gordon, Saul Tschernichovsky, Yacov Kahan, David Frischman, Zalman Schneur, Yehuda Halevy and others.

My maternal grandfather, Aaron Rosenblum, who was a fanatic *Gerer Hassid*, did not quite like all this. He insisted that my parents send me to a *Yeshiva*, so I was enrolled in the *Yeshiva Machzikei Hadat* in Lodz. On the other hand, my mother, a graduate of a Russian *gymnasium*, wanted her children to have a formal general education. My older sister attended a Polish *gymnasium*, but a debate developed over me. Finally it was agreed that until *bar mitzvah* I would study at the *Yeshiva*, while at the same time I would have a private tutor for secular subjects. After *bar mitzvah* I would take the examinations for entering the *gymnasium*.

Because of the economic crisis of the second decade of this century, several companies to which my father had sold textiles went bankrupt. He lost heavily and decided to liquidate his factory. He took a job with a large textile firm in Lodz.

I recall an incident of that period which left a permanent imprint on our lives. One day grandfather came to visit us, which was a rare occurrence. Through the open door I heard a heated debate. My father was telling grandfather that he had received a proposal from his employer to go to America as a textile expert, to purchase certain materials. Grandfather roared against this: "Leizer, don't you dare go! I'll be ashamed to come to *shtibl* (a Hassidic house of prayer)! What will they think of me if my son-in-law goes off to America?"

Knowing that my father was in financial trouble, he offered him two thousand rubles, just so he would not leave for America. But my father proudly replied that he did not want to be a beggar. My mother, who was present, pleaded tearfully to father that he should not go to America, and he promised them both that he would stay home. But that was not the end of that.

A few weeks later—this was in 1913—father came home and declared that because of the textile crisis, he had to go to the Czech city of Brunn to learn the art of making tulle. He went off, and a few weeks later we received a letter from him—not from Brunn but from New York. He had left after the *Shavuot* festival and returned in time for the High Holidays.

The following year, father went to America again. It was the summer of 1914, and he was stuck there when the war broke out. At the invitation of his cousin, Samuel Greenford, a wealthy real estate broker in Montreal, he went on to Canada. In partnership with a Galician Jew named Katz, my father opened a blanket factory. When Canada entered the war, Mr. Katz, who was an Austrian citizen, was interned and my father remained the owner of the factory. He sent us money through Switzerland, and when the war ended he sold the factory in order to return to Zgierz. He was sure that his wife would not want to come to Canada.

On the way, father stopped in London, from where he wired that he was coming home. To his surprise, mother telegraphed back: "Don't come. We would rather go to Canada." This was late in 1919 when I was already in Eretz Israel. However, that is another story which I intend to complete later, for it is at the heart of my memoirs.

At the beginning of the war, with father stranded in Canada, mother decided that the family should go to Zgierz, to live in the house which father had inherited. The house was shared with father's elder sister, Yachtsha. By moving in, we saved on rent. Until my *bar mitzvah*, I studied at the *beth hamidrash* in Zgierz. On passing my examinations, I entered a Lodz *gymnasium*, to which I went daily by streetcar.

Now, years later, the earliest impressions of my childhood

float into my consciousness, events that happened when I was four or five years old. The first recollection is of the year 1905, when the first Russian Revolution broke out. Revolutionary shocks reverberated over the entire Russian empire and also reached the city of Lodz, a workers' center full of revolutionaries. Our house on Tzegelnyana street was U-shaped, with a front and two side wings. On the right side of the courtyard, surrounded by a fence, was a warehouse full of scrap iron. One day the courtyard was invaded by Cossacks with rifles and drawn swords. Looking through the window, I saw their wild horses leaping over the fence as the Cossacks fired their guns. Years later I found out that in the basement of our house was the headquarters of *Poale Zion*.

Two other incidents of that period were traumatic experiences. We were living at 56 Tzegelnyana street in Lodz. My parents had bought me a new coat for Passover. I was very proud of it, as it was very handsome and made me look like a big boy. I paraded around in the new garment, to show off before my friends. Suddenly, a stranger entered the courtyard, came up to me and said he was a tailor who had sewn the garment. He had to fix something on it. He led me up a few stairs of the front part of the house and put me on the windowsill. He tore off a button and with a swift maneuver removed my coat. He told me to wait until he went to his shop to sew on the button. I sat and waited, a long wait, until I realized that he had stolen my coat. I shrieked and ran home to my father, who comforted me and bought me a new one.

A second experience was more dramatic and could have been tragic. My grandparents lived in a large house on the opposite side of the street. Once I went to visit them with my younger brother, Yossel, who was then three-and-a-half years old. Mother admonished me to hold his hand and watch carefully when we crossed the street. Suddenly, Yossel slipped away and started to cross by himself. He fell in the path of an oncoming coach. From all sides, pedestrians yelled and several men grabbed Yossel and rushed him into our house. A doctor was summoned. It turned out that Yossel had been only mildly hurt by the wagon wheels, which had rubber tires; the road was, fortunately, paved with wooden blocks. However, I knew none of this and when I saw my brother lying under the wheels I panicked and ran into the house. I crawled under the sofa, where I fell asleep. All day my mother searched for me. Finally, when my father came from his factory, he spotted my feet sticking out. Delicately, he pulled me out from under the sofa. To reassure me that all was well, he took me to Yossel's bed and showed me that nothing serious had happened to him. But to this day I can not free myself of that picture of Yossel under the wheels, and I shall never forget the sensation of hiding a whole day under a sofa, suffering from an overwhelming sense of guilt.

A third incident, but of an entirely different nature, took place much later. I was then ten or eleven years old. The chief rabbi of Lodz, Eliahu Chaim Meisel, died, and elections were to be held to choose a new chief rabbi. The Jewish community was turned into a battlefield. The pious Jews divided into two camps: on one side was the *Agudah* and the *Gerer Hassidim*, who backed the candidacy of the rabbi of Radom, Eliezer Treistman. In the opposition was the *Alexanderer Hassidim* and the *Mizrachi*, who favored Rabbi Yechezel Lifschitz of Kalish. The electioneering was so bitter that *Hassidic* voters were brought to the polls by coach. My family, of course, was energetically involved in the campaign. I, a big boy, was assigned to drive around in a coach to help bring out the vote for "our" candidate. I felt highly important, sitting up front with the driver, riding around Lodz to deliver the *Hassidim* to the polling places.

Just as the two previous incidents—involving my coat and my brother—remain as painful memories, the driving around Lodz in a coach full of *Hassidim* remains a pleasant moment that flatters my ego. the *Gerer Hassidim* won. Rabbi Treistman was elected.

LEAVING HOME

BEFORE THE FIRST WORLD WAR, ZGIERZ HAD A NUMBER OF Jewish youth organizations, but by decree of the Russian government they could not be political. The young people had to join non-political sports clubs or cultural circles which functioned around the library. During the first months of the war, as the Germans conquered Lodz and other parts of Russian Poland, radical changes transpired.

The Germans permitted ideological organizations and a group of us at the local school of commerce, which was strongly Russified, and of the Jewish *gymnasium* and other schools in Lodz, decided to form a youth organization that would differ from the existing ones. We were mostly children of well-to-do homes. Not knowing exactly what we wanted, we began to study avidly the programs of other youth organizations, which then existed in various European countries. For example, there was the Sokal of the Czechs and the Pathfinders in Germany as well as the scouts of Baden-Powell in England.

After long debates, we decided to establish a sort of Jewish scout movement, which, in addition to the general scouting program would bear a distinct Jewish character: the members would also study Hebrew, Jewish history, the geography of Palestine and the life of the Jewish pioneers in Eretz Israel. The chief purpose, however, was to implant the impulse to ascend, personally, to Eretz Israel. Since I knew Hebrew and

41

Jewish history, I was assigned the task of teaching these two subjects, as well as Palestinography.

Similar Jewish scout groups began to blossom in Lodz and the surrounding region at the same time. The headquarters of the organization was located in Lodz, and some Zgierz leaders became members of the central leadership body.

In 1917, the year of the Balfour Declaration, Jews throughout the world, but especially those in the cities and towns of Eastern Europe, were seized with the fervor and belief that the Jewish people was on the threshold of realizing the two-thousand-year-old dream of returning to Zion, of coming home to the ancient Jewish homeland. This spirit also animated our scout movement and aroused in some of our leaders the desire to go on *Aliya*. One could not discuss this idea openly because we were still under the German occupation. We lived with the hope that immediately after the war's end, when the routes of the world would be safely open, we would freely realize our dream.

A year later, in 1918, the Jewish scout movements in Russian-Poland which had sprouted all over, united with kindred organizations in Austria, which were called *Hashomer Hatzair*, and the general organization assumed this name.

The central headquarters of *Hashomer Hatzair* was located in the Bet Am community center in Lodz. The local unit was also situated there, together with a variety of other Zionist groups. In addition there was a large library. During the war a non-profit kitchen was set up by the *Zeire Zion*. Because of the constant fear of pogroms, a self-defense unit was maintained at the Bet Am.

The need for a self-defense unit was made clear by an incident that almost ended in tragedy. In the final months of the war, the Germans began to confiscate all kinds of metals, which were needed by their war industry, especially copper and bronze. Among other things, they confiscated the large copper bell of the Catholic church in the old section of Lodz. A rumor inspired by anti-Semites spread among the Poles that the Jews had done it. Hordes of Polish peasants flocked into Lodz from the nearby villages, bent upon attacking the Jews. The Jews saw the necessity of organizing themselves against impending attack, and all segments, ranging from the religious and the Zionists to the Bund joined forces. Butchers armed with knives also joined the ranks.

An emergency meeting was held in the Bet Am. It was decided to post armed members at every point that might be attacked. The president of the Lodz city council was a Pole, and the vice-president was a Jew named Dr. Jesse Rosenblatt. When the Germans arrested the president, Dr. Rosenblatt was elected to serve as acting president. Quickly, he went to the old market place, where thousands of peasants had gathered, stood on top of a coach and addressed the throng which was seething with anti-Semitic venom. He explained to them that the Germans, not the Jews, had removed the bell. Eventually he convinced the peasants, and a bloody battle was averted.

When it was realized that the Germans were losing the war, a new menace faced the Jews of Lodz. Secret Polish military groups called Woyskufka, appeared in the open and rumors began to circulate that they would fight for Polish independence—beginning with assaults on Jews. Just then, two Jewish leaders, one who returned from Russia to Poland, Yitzhak Greenbaum, and the other, Dr. Yehoshua Gottlieb, toured the country with a political message. They reached Lodz where they addressed a huge mass meeting in the Jewish Theatre on Constantine street. That night the theatre was jammed with thousands of people. Our self-defense discovered that units of the Woyskufka were preparing for a bloody attack upon the Jews when they would be leaving the theatre. We quickly organized the students within the defense corps, who were armed with revolvers, and formed a ring around the theatre. With loud voices, so that the Poles would know clearly where matters stood, the students yelled, "Just let them dare!" The heroic Poles heard the warning and melted away.

At last came November 11, 1918. Armistice. We had lived with the hope that on this day we could commence the realization of our dream, to begin our journey to the land of Israel. We convened a secret conference of the *Hashomer Hatzair* leadership. Our plan was to reach Eretz Israel the same way that the first *Biluim* did, through Odessa, but for various reasons that was not possible. At a secret meeting, we decided to send an emissary to Vienna, to explore the possibility of using an Italian port. On November 20, one of our members, named Marcus, set out for Vienna. Six days later he returned with a positive assessment. The leaders of the Zionist organization in Lodz opposed the idea, saying that it was a dangerous route, since the area was still in a state of war, but we decided to disregard their warning and to go ahead.

The decisive meeting was held November 30. With elation, we adopted the definitive resolution to set forth on December 3. We had fourteen members, and to this day I have kept the list of names of all those who actually went along. They were all students or graduates of *gymnasiums*. Some were from Lodz and some from Zgierz: Ceshek (Zadik) Rosenthal, Aryeh-Leib Rubinstein (myself), Abraham Greenberg, Nathan Spivak, Jacob Dombrovski, Tuvia Altman, Yehuda Rubin, Jacob Slomowitz, Chaim Luria, Jacob Skosovski, Simcha Grosbard, Zelig Reichert, Besem (whose first name I have forgotten), and Marcus.

We were all from more or less affluent families and did not depart empty-handed. Each received from his family some money. We were also quite practical, and took along some food—flour, sugar, cereals and canned meat. The group leader was my close friend Skosovski, an excellent speaker and organizer. Another close friend was Zelig Reichert. Ceshek Rosenthal hailed from an assimilated family and did not know any Yiddish. Rubin spoke French, and we figured that this would come in handy along the road.

On December 1 we assembled for photographs. On the same day our joyous mood was disturbed by a letter from

Vienna—telling us not to come as the chances of our continuing from there were not bright. We received a similar warning through our own Zionist organization in Lodz. The only one to encourage us at that critical juncture was Dr. Jesse Rosenblatt. We ignored the warnings from Vienna and the pessimistic words of the Zionist leadership of Lodz. We were too enthusiastic for such alarms to have any influence on us and we proceeded according to plan. On December 2 Jewish students staged a farewell banquet in our honor at the Bet Am. It was an unforgettable evening, attended by all the Jewish councilmen of Lodz, representatives of the women's organizations, Zionist leaders, representatives of the *Zeire Zion* and *Poale Zion*, some teachers, students and others.

Dr. Rosenblatt chaired the evening. Speakers representing the participating organizations greeted the *Halutzim. Miriam*, a women's group, presented to each of us a small *Tanach*, inscribed with good wishes for a safe journey. One of the most impressive speeches was that delivered by the sister of Menachem, the leader of *Hashomer Hatzair*, who was at that time a student at the Cracow University. She ended her remarks with the assurance: "Should you for any reason be forced to come back, do not be unhappy. We will receive you with open arms." She sounded like a mother talking to her own children.

To comprehend the meaning of her words, one must take into consideration the conditions under which we departed. The trip was risky. None of us knew the way. We knew nothing of the countries we were to cross. We were not even sure after we reached an Italian port that we could get a ship, and whether after we got aboard we would debark in the land of Israel. But we were all soaring on our ideals which would by magic remove all these obstacles and pave the way to our destination.

We divided into two groups as we did not want to be too visible in the sight of Polish authorities. It was uncertain whether the Polish regime, which had just constituted a free

Poland, would allow young people to leave the country.

I left Lodz the morning of December 3 with the first group, while the second departed in the afternoon. We all wore student caps with a Polish eagle pinned in front, like students at Cracow University. Friends came to the station to bid us farewell, but to avoid making too much of a scene, they stayed outside.

Aboard the train I placed my valise on a baggage rack, but as there were no seats I went to the next car. Because of this, I had a lot of trouble a few hours later, a foretaste of other misadventures, a sign that the journey would not be so easy. Polish controllers boarded the train at Czenstochowa and inspected the baggage. Since my valise was locked and had no claimant at hand, they removed it from the train, which continued without it. As the train began to move, my friends told me what happened. In order to rescue the valise, which contained all my clothes and food, I dropped off at the next station, Zambkovitza, and took a train back to Czenstochowa. The car was almost empty and its windows were broken. A soldier seated near me said that the Poles had waged a pogrom that day in Lemberg. This was one of the first patriotic manifestations of the Polish people, expressing their joy at winning a national independence. Besides sitting in a cold, empty car, I spent a few miserable hours in terror.

Arriving at the Czenstochowa station, I located the stationmaster and told him my story. My valise was indeed there, and they opened it in my presence. The luggage was mostly filled with food, but there was one item which raised the suspicion of the stationmaster that I was some kind of spy. It was a lorgnette which I had gotten from a German officer, who had taken it from a French officer at the front. The stationmaster examined me: "How did you get a military lorgnette?" I explained that it was not a military lorgnette but a civilian one, and showed him the French inscription, which he did not understand. It was apparent that he was not interested in my lorgnette but in something else: my food supply. He returned the glasses and helped himself to some of my bread and sugar.

I waited for the next train on which the second half of our group was to arrive. At the station a gang of hoodlums harassed the Jews with insults and threats. I was embittered by all this, for I had sympathized with the Poles in their struggle for independence. We hoped it would bring an end to 150 years of enslavement by neighboring countries and that Polish soil would no longer be occupied by foreign powers. But on the morning after liberation, just as the Polish eagle spread its wings in freedom, many Poles had nothing better in mind than to persecute their Jewish compatriots.

At last I heard the distant whistle of a locomotive. The Lodz train pulled into the station and I spotted my comrades. I called out to one of them, "Simcha!" When they saw me they were scared, suspecting that something bad had happened. I told them the whole story of the valise and why I had come back to Czenstochowa. When they heard that the stationmaster had taken some of my food they began to hide their own provisions.

At the next station, Zambkowitza, we again split into two groups. One took a direct train to Vienna and the other headed toward Cracow. I was attached to the latter unit. We had the address of our comrade Menachem, who received us heartily and we slept at his place. At night he led us into a room full of weapons belonging to the Jewish self-defense. For a minute we were overcome with terror. Suddenly the door opened and a man entered, pointing a flashlight at us. We were sure we had been discovered by a Polish agent, but it transpired that he was our own comrade, Chaim Luria.

The next day we visited historic sights in Cracow. We saw castles and other imposing buildings which we had known from photographs in our school books: the famous *Sukenitza*, the Cathedral of St. Maria, the Wawell Castle adjacent to the Cathedral of St. Wenceslas where Polish kings were buried. But we were more eager to see Jewish places. We visited the Cracow synagogue where we experienced a bizarre incident. It was Hannukah, and on the Balemer, where the Torah is read, was a menorah with the Hannukah candles aglow. A Hassidic congregant prayed so fervently he bowed too closely to the menorah and his fur-trimmed had caught fire. The other worshippers quickly extinguished the flames.

From the synagogue we went to the cemetery, which was dotted with ancient Jewish tombstones. We located the grave of Rabbi Moshe Isserlis, the sixteenth-century scholar. At noon we ate lunch at the Jewish students' kitchen. Then Menachem took us to the station where we were able to take the train to Vienna. Not far from the station we were halted by the Polish secret police, to whom we appeared suspicious. Menachem explained that we were students and we were allowed to go free.

To escape the vigilance of the police, Menachem led us in a roundabout way through the baggage room directly to the tracks. On the platform, women were dispensing coffee and rolls to the passengers, especially the Polish soldiers. We also enjoyed this treat.

After saying goodbye to Menachem, we piled aboard the train, without tickets. In those days there was chaos, and the sale of tickets was not well organized, most of the passengers riding free.

When the train started to move we breathed freely. It was late at night. The train stopped at Ludenberg, where we spent the night. Next morning we covered a long stretch of Austria and approached the capital of the former Austro-Hungarian empire, now the capital of Austria, Vienna. The train pulled into the cavernous, well-lit station. We collected our belongings and got off.

It was a frosty night. We were tired and cold, but above all, we were sleepy and did not know where to turn first. Not far from the station was the National Guard headquarters, the Austrian militia. We didn't take too long to decide to go inside. Fate was kind to us. One of the guards was Jewish. Seeing who we were, he didn't make a fuss, but told us we could sleep on the floor.

Early in the morning, Austrian officers came along and looked us over with suspicion. After learning our identity, they allowed us to go into the city. We took our packs and passed through the station—we were in Vienna!

VIENNA

WE YOUNGSTERS FROM THE SMALL TOWN OF ZGIERZ, OR even of the larger city of Lodz, were mystified by the glamor of Vienna, the elegant metropolis. In our fantasy, it was the center of waltzes and royal ballets, of "dancing congresses" and of magnificent palaces and monuments.

But on that frigid morning, when we emerged from the railway station all these beauties meant nothing to us. Even in this gay city, we were at once enveloped by a somber spirit. Our mood was so depressed that some of our comrades did not wish to travel any further. There were also those who, upon hearing of the incessant pogroms against the Jews of Lemberg and other places, wanted to join the self-defense and return to protect the endangered Jewish communities. But these were only transitory feelings and doubts; we got rid of them quickly.

We called on Dr. Scharf, chairman of the Viennese Zionist Organization. He welcomed us graciously and this helped dispel the gloom in our hearts. Dr. Scharf took us to a well-lit coffee house, where we told him our plans, and he promised to help. He agreed that we should proceed to Italy, to a port where we might find a ship.

Friday evening we went to the Great Synagogue of Vienna, where we heard a sermon by Rabbi Professor Zvi Chajes. We asked Dr. Scharf to arrange a meeting between us and

Rabbi Chajes, but the meeting turned out to be a big let-down. He opposed our plan of going through Yugoslavia to Italy, because of the uncertain situation which would endanger us. In general he did not believe that we would find a ship, and warned us that we might be stranded on the road.

We left Rabbi Chajes in a disappointed frame of mind, but not in resignation. We were bent on overcoming any passing moment of despair, determined to ignore all potential dangers and to press forward. Next day, in the general kitchen where we had our meals, we met a Roumanian Jew named Marcus, who declared that he wanted to join our group. We accepted him because he knew several languages and we thought that he would be quite useful.

With the assistance of Dr. Scharf we made contact with a former Italian consul, who had been interned in Vienna during the war. He listened to our plans and offered to give us a letter that would help us.

During the few days we spent in Vienna we took the opportunity to see the marvelous sights of the capital: the Wienerwald, the castles and the sculptures and the gilded roofs, the cathedrals, including the largest Gothic church in Europe, and the grand plazas with their monuments. We also strolled along the banks of the Danube which has inspired so many composers and poets. We were young students and had an insatiable appetite for art and architectural wonders. But stronger than our curiosity about the city was our impatience to move on, and we restlessly counted the minutes until we could take our bags and resume our journey.

On December 7 we boarded a trolley heading for the railway station. The car was jammed with passengers, and since we were foreigners, weighed down with luggage, we were simply pushed off. We had to walk the rest of the way, dragging our heavy burdens. At last we reached the station and boarded the train which was going south, in the direction of Trieste. I write as though this was an easy trip, but it was not so.

51

In those days, in that part of Europe, there was a vast migration of peoples. Hordes were transferring from Trieste to Vienna, and from Vienna to Trieste. The railway cars were packed—hundreds of passengers jammed the aisles, sat on the steps, and even rode on the roofs. As we came closer to Yugoslavia, we left the train at a station, and bought tickets for Trieste.

The new train that we boarded was full of repatriated Italians, who had been interned in Austria and who were now travelling in organized groups under the wing of Italian officials. We remembered that our new member Marcus was a linguist and we asked him to speak to the Italians to get their help for our journey. For various reasons, Marcus refused and we began to look at him with suspicion.

On the way, the train halted and we had to get off. It seems that during the war the tracks had been torn up. We had to shoulder our packs, and go by foot to Murenhausen and Spielfeld where we mounted a freight train. After riding through Austria and Yugoslavia, we approached the Italian border.

The same evening we reached a small railway station, Leudz. Here we again had an unexpected experience. Earlier, we saw that the leader of the repatriated Italians was looking at us askance. When we came to Leudz, we were commanded to get off the train. The Italian repatriates continued further but we were ushered into a cattlecar whose floor was covered with quicklime. The car was pushed up a hill and stood there, isolated, far from the station. We figured out that we had been interned, as outside the car was an armed Italian soldier who kept an eye on us.

Since none of us could speak Italian, and our new member Marcus had refused to talk, we couldn't communicate with the soldier and didn't know what was going to happen. Meanwhile, night fell and we had no choice but to lie down on our baggage and try to sleep. It was cold and uncomfortable. Early in the morning, when the first rays of light began to enter the cattlecar, we opened the door. The first thing we saw was the armed guard who had stood by all night, watching over us.

With the help of hand signals, we told him we wanted water. He smiled at us, folded his arms and said only one word: "Niente." His face told us more than that unfamiliar Italian word. We looked around and saw that our car was perched on a rocky hill in the middle of a wilderness. We were surrounded by bare mountains. It was obvious that even if we took our packs and tried to escape we would not find our way. Since we could not communicate with the soldier, we hit upon the idea of faking illness and demanding a doctor. We calculated that a doctor, being an educated person, might know languages besides Italian. On the alert, we waited for the changing of the guards. When the soldier on night duty was relieved, we began to yell "Doctor! Doctor!" We assumed that doctor was an international word and he would understand, but to be sure we began to gesticulate—one of us held his head, another his belly and a third coughed violently. We kept repeating: "Doctor! Doctor!"

Our plan worked. The soldier got the idea and reported to headquarters that the young men were sick. It didn't take long before a military doctor came. He understood a little French and we thought he would be able to converse with our French-speaking Rubin. Only then did we tell the truth; Rubin told him that we didn't need medicine but only wanted to talk to the military commander to find our why we were being kept isolated in this cattlecar. The doctor promised to get an answer and he kept his word. Soon, a patrol came to escort us back to the railway station at Leudz, and handed us over to the military commander.

The commander's French was weak but sufficient to convey to Rubin that the authorities considered us spies! Rubin argued with him at length, explaining who we were and that we had no intention of remaining in Italy. All we wanted was to reach a port so that we could sail to Eretz Israel. The commander laughed at this. He didn't believe us.

Who knows what might have happened if a miracle had not occurred. By chance, at the depot there was an Italian Jew, Dr. Freund, who was returning to Trieste. We asked him to intervene on our behalf, to try to convince the commander that we were not dangerous spies but a simple group of young Jews whose sole interest was to get to Eretz Israel as fast as possible.

To us, Dr. Freund looked like a savior angel. He argued with the military commander a long time, assuring him that the Jewish community of Rome would put up guarantees if we were released. It was interesting to note that while all this was going on the Roumanian, Marcus, sat by silently, as though with a mouthful of water. We had taken him into our circle because of his linguistic prowess, and now that he was really needed, he kept his mouth shut. Our suspicions were aroused, and we decided to get rid of him at the first opportunity.

The Italian commander became more amenable. We showed him our papers and asked for two things: first, for something to drink, as we had not had a drop of liquid for almost twenty-four hours; secondly, and more important, a temporary place to stay, until our permits to go further would arrive. Both requests were granted. We were served coffee and biscuits. Then we were led into the officers' barracks, where there were beds and a stove. The stove was out of order, as we found out when we lit it and were rewarded with a coat of soot and smoke. Still, the stove was a godsend, and the room gradually got warmer. We heated some of our food and ate a cooked meal for a change.

Next day, a soldier led us to the commander. We were afraid of two possibilities: either we would be arrested as spies or he would send us back to Vienna. Neither happened. Dr. Freund had really informed the Jewish community in Rome and they had sent a telegram with their guarantee that

54

we were not spies. They requested that we be allowed to proceed.

A guard led us to the train and told us to board the third-class carriage. But here, too, we were destined to suffer some uneasy moments. After we were seated a couple of soldiers ordered us to collect our luggage and get off the train. Where were they taking us? Back to the commander? To jail? No, they took us to another car, second class. It seems that the commander had decided to give us a treat: instead of the hard seats in third class we would have the comfortable accommodations of second class. Nevertheless, it took some time before we calmed down and we began to laugh gaily.

Our laughter did not last long. Terror struck again. When the train began to move, we noticed that it was going backward. Had we been fooled? Were we being returned to Vienna?

It didn't matter that the train was only being shunted to another track. We sat staring out the windows, and we calmed down only when we saw in the distance the blue waters of the Mediterranean. We not only calmed down but sprang up with tremendous joy. At last! Our goal was in sight. Soon we would be in Trieste, where we could board a ship to Alexandria and from there it was only a short hop to the Promised Land!

This sounded so simple in theory, but in reality things were entirely different.

TRIESTE

THE TRAIN CHUGGED INTO TRIESTE ON DECEMBER 13 IN THE Middle of the night. Our plan was to go right into the city, but the first upset occurred immediately. The station officials informed us, half in sign language, that we were not allowed to enter the city and that we would have to sleep in the station.

Luckily, an Italian officer who had ridden with us in the last car watched the scene. He began to argue with the officials who finally relented and allowed us to get out of the depot.

Now the question was: where to go? With difficulty we located a small, cheap hotel and for the first time since we left Vienna we could stretch out on beds and rest our bones.

Next morning we went to town, to call on the local office of the Zionist Organization. On the way, we caught sight of the great port, which was the object of a struggle between Italy and Yugoslavia. As we strolled along the broad, modern streets, we viewed Trieste as an Italian city. All the restaurants were Italian, all passersby spoke Italian. After Vienna, Trieste was the second most imposing city, with its bright avenues and impressive buildings and churches.

We inquired about the street where the Zionist office was located. We found it and met the chairman, Mr. Dlugatch. We introduced ourselves and he received us cordially. The first news we received from him was not pleasant: no ships went directly from Trieste to Jaffa or Alexandria. Dlugatch told us we would have to be very patient, a word that we were to hear frequently in the ensuing days, weeks, months. But patience was not a virtue that we possessed in abundance. We were restless and wanted to move on quickly to our destination.

From Herr Dlugatch we also learned that we were not the only *Halutzim* in Trieste. There was also a group from Bendin, Poland. He gave us their address and we looked them up. The Bendiner group had taken rooms in a much nicer, more expensive hotel. In addition, there were several more *Halutz* groups waiting in Trieste.

After visiting Herr Dlugatch and the Bendiners, we returned to our hotel. We saw the difficulties ahead of us and decided to be a bit more practical, to organize our living on a healthier economic basis. Not knowing how long our wanderings would take, we had to be careful with our capital. We organized a sort of commune, pooling all our food supplies. We decided to cook our own meals and I was put in charge of the food inventory.

Meanwhile we had some free time and we were eager to explore the city. From our school days, we knew something about Italy, its cities, its art treasures and its history. Now we could see the great port on the northern Adriatic coast. The most interesting aspect of Trieste was its harbor with all the fleets anchored at the docks. The port seethed with action and noise, it was alive, and we struck up a close acquaintance with it as we came every day to poke around and try to find a ship that might be going to Alexandria or Jaffa.

The churches, and especially the imposing cathedral adorned with countless mosaics and sculptures, impressed us immensely. Among the most colorful sights was the market, where fishermen stood by barrels full of live fish that they had caught themselves. In the center of the city was a museum filled with Italian and non-Italian art as well as archeological finds. We walked the streets as though we were intoxicated, drinking in the pictures and sounds of the Italian language which sounded like the arias of an Italian opera.

But above all, of course, was our interest in Jewish life. The first Friday evening we went to the synagogue, which surprised us, it was so large. It was built in ancient Babylonian style, with a rich marble facade and bronze doors adorned with tablets inscribed with the Ten Commandments. The interior of the synagogue was embellished with marble columns. The chandeliers and the *bimah* were decorated with dark bronze. The Holy Ark had huge bronze doors, and when the beadle, dressed like a soldier in the old Napoleonic army, pulled back the curtain and opened the doors, we stood charmed by the glorious sight, the Torah scrolls topped by golden crowns and rich gold-braided mantles.

In one of the large halls behind the synagogue we saw a library with glass bookcases filled with hundreds of leather-bound volumes and shelves laden with precious manuscripts.

It was the first time we had ever seen an organ in a synagogue. Another surprise was that there were Christian girls singing in the choir.

We met the spiritual head of the Trieste synagogue, Rabbi Israel Zoller. He was the same Dr. Zoller who later became chief Rabbi of Italy. During the second World War, he was given a safe haven in the Vatican. The Jewish world was shocked when he eventually converted to Catholicism.

That evening, however, Dr. Zoller was very cordial and expressed a desire to be of help. His promises were not empty phrases. Our leader, Jacob Skosovski, through the intervention of Dr. Zoller, was able to contact the governor of Trieste, who was of great assistance, not to find a ship but to get transportation to Genoa, a few weeks later.

We had hoped to be in Trieste only a day or two before sailing off, but that was not to be. Hearing that other *Halutzim* from Polish towns were in Trieste, also seeking a way to Eretz Israel, we decided to hold a conference of all the groups at the Hotel Palast. We elected a joint leadership and

58

our comrade Skosovski was elected chairman of the entire body. The meeting took place on December 16. The same day, we decided to eliminate from our group Marcus, the Roumanian. His behavior was such that we had no confidence in him; we felt that he was hiding something from us and that he could cause trouble.

On December 17, the chairman of the Trieste Zionist Organization, Herr Dlugatch, who had been so friendly, suddenly announced that he no longer had any obligations to us as we did not have an official letter from the Zionist Council of Vienna. This cold, bureaucratic declaration hit us like an icy stream of water but did not dampen our enthusiasm nor deter us from proceeding toward our goal. Gradually we had become aware that Herr Dlugatch could do little for us anyway, that he was misleading us with false promises. Once he told us that he had received a letter from Nahum Sokolow about our case and that on Wednesday, December 26, we would certainly get going. Nothing came of that promise.

We saw that other groups were acting on better advice than ours. For example, a group that had come from Radom and went right away to the port of Fiume. Some of our members therefore suggested that we should pack up and leave Trieste, since the situation was hopeless. But this would have been an illegal act and the idea was rejected.

The problem of our departure began to drag on and on. Afraid that our finances would soon be exhausted, we decided that it would be good if we could earn some money. Some of us began to peddle matches and herring, others earned money by trading in currencies.

The Italian police kept an eye on us. One of our group, Spivak, was arrested one evening. Three others noticed that they were being followed by Italian secret agents. We decided to be very cautious and not engage in any illegal activities.

There was stormy weather in Trieste. On December 26 a severe north wind, the *bora*, hit the Adriatic coast. It was so severe that the heavy ropes were tied to the walls of houses, for pedestrians to hold on to as they fought their way along the streets or they could be blown away. That day, we planned to make our usual visit to the port to look for a sailing vessel, but the storm was so fierce that we had to cancel the trip.

Many Jewish residents of Trieste heard of us and wished to help. I remember two of them: Abramson and Mandelzweig. Not only the Jews of Trieste but the Jews of the whole world knew about us. There were articles in the Jewish press in many countries.

One day our comrade Luria received a letter from Lodz asking whether it was true that some of the group had died on the way and that some were hospitalized. We used the good offices of Dr. Freund, and each of us wrote a letter to our parents to reassure them that all was well, that we were in good health and that we expected to go on with our journey very soon. These were consoling words for our parents, but we were in a depressed mood.

On December 26 the Bendin group protested—they were dissatisfied with the leadership of our comrade, Skosovski. Adding to all these troubles was the arrival of a fellow named Kreilisheim, a Hungarian middle-aged Jew, shrewd, with diamond-studded rings on the fingers of both hands. He persuaded us that he wanted to be of help, claiming that he knew a captain of a vessel who had promised to take along about thirty people from our joint group to Alexandria. The Bendin group swallowed his story. It turned out that Kreilisheim was a plain swindler, that he had taken some money from the Bendiners and divided it with the captain. We informed the police, and Kreilisheim, together with the captain, were arrested. No money was found on them, and we soft-hearted Jews pleaded that they should not be punished too harshly.

That was a side episode, which merely indicates what we were going through. During one of the general meetings of the group, a charge was brought that the Italian Jews were worried that some of us were dealing in money. We gave our sacred word that we would not allow this to go on.

We had other troubles. Shliamovitz developed an earache. We were worried that this might be contagious but the ailment turned out to be minor. But henceforth we paid stricter attention to sanitation, to regular bathing, and in general tried to avoid exposure to disease.

On the night of December 31 there was a general gathering of all the Jewish students in Trieste. We celebrated with them the arrival of the New Year, 1919, although there was really no good reason to be happy.

We began to rebel against Herr Dlugatch, who was responsible for helping us, since he was head of the Zionist organization. But he had done nothing. On January 4 news came that the Radom group which had gone to Fiume had already left from there for Palestine. This made us even more restless and impatient. Sunday, January 5, we sent a member of the Sosnowitz group to Fiume to explore the situation.

Meanwhile, we implemented another plan. We went to the Spanish consul, who represented a neutral country, and we asked him to issue stateless passports to us, as we did not want to display our German passports. We also asked him to write on our passports that we were Hebreo-Russo-Pollaki. The reason for this unusual formulation was that Hebreo would show that we were going to Eretz Israel, Russo, that we were not Poles, making us subject to being drafted into the Polish Army, and Pollaki would show that we were not communists, as in those days the name "Russian" immediately brought an association with Bolshevism. The Spanish consul was persuaded to do our bidding, and he issued the passes. From then on we each carried a document with the tri-national identification. With these new, somewhat peculiar passports, we felt much better.

Our final days in Trieste were a mixture of hot and cold, of black and white, of hope and bitter disappointment. For example, on January 10, Skosovski stated that on the day after next we would leave for Eretz Israel. The night prior to our supposed departure, we held a session, heard impassioned speeches and danced and sang the *Hatikvah*.

On January 11 we released our hotel rooms, but it transpired that the whole thing had fizzled out. Our mood was so bad that some of our members, Marcus from Lodz and several from Lentschitz, couldn't bear it any longer and decided to go back to Poland. Without too much ceremony, we quietly bade them goodbye.

Throughout this entire period, the governor of Trieste frowned upon us, and when the scandal with Kreilisheim broke, he suspected us all and wanted to get rid of us as quickly as possible. He arranged for our trip to Genoa, where supposedly it was easier to find a boat. He succeeded in getting us free rides. On January 15, a month after our arrival in Trieste, during which we had accomplished nothing, we boarded the train for Genoa. We had fresh hopes that there, in the port where Columbus was born, we would have as much luck as the discoverer of America.

GENOA

ON THE ROAD FROM TRIESTE TO GENOA WE HAD TO CHANGE
trains at Mestra. It was a fascinating ride. As the train passed
forested mountains and went through long tunnels, we enjoyed the colorful landscape of northern Italy, and when it
slowed down gradually, we knew that we were about to reach
Genoa. It was six weeks since we had left home.

Our first act was to find a hotel, where we could deposit
our luggage and rest up. We found a cheap place called "Har-
monia."

Following our usual routine, we went to the synagogue to
look for Jews. But it wasn't easy to find a synagogue. After
some communication difficulty, we got a passerby to help us.
He led us into side streets, and in a dirty alley, he pointed to
a nondescript building, saying that this was the synagogue. It
wasn't what we had expected. It was an ordinary house, with
a cross hanging at the entrance. The synagogue itself was in
the attic, and when we clambered up the dirty stairway and
knocked on the door, a beadle appeared. He didn't want to
admit us. Since it was late afternoon, we waited until a *min-
yan* would assemble and then we met our first Jews. But it
was a confrontation that brought few results.

We returned to the hotel, which was one of the shabbiest
in Genoa, and decided to go the very next morning to the
port to hunt for a ship. There we encountered a situation

that almost ended in bloodshed. Joseph Millet, a musician in our group, who boasted a trim beard, noticed an Italian girl near the port. Apparently under the influence of the romantic notions gleaned from Italian operas, he made an advance. Suddenly an Italian sailor materialized out of nowhere and with a drawn knife he jumped on our would-be Don Juan. We barely held the sailor back, and Millet escaped unharmed. The incident was over in a flash, but it taught us something about the temperament of Italian sailors.

We wandered around the docks and looked with dreamy eyes at the sea. On the distant shore was the land of our hopes—but where was the ship that would bring us there?

On January 18, together with Skosovski, I went to the rabbi at the Central Synagogue of Genoa. We emerged from the slum quarters of the city and strode along the broad thoroughfares. The rabbi welcomed us cordially and heard our tale sympathetically, admiring our idealism. He promised to do all he could.

We had already learned from past experience in Trieste that there was a wide gap between words and deeds. The first thing we knew, after the conversation with the rabbi, was that we had to shore up our patience. Furthermore, we would have to economize even more on food and cigarettes. We ate lunch at a popular restaurant, *Cucino Populare*, where prices were low and the food was not *de luxe*.

One of our comrades from Radom had been a barber, and he trimmed and shaved us. We did our own laundry and pressing and other chores in order to save money.

Our leadership group was very active in Genoa. On January 20 we held a meeting at the Central Synagogue. Skosovski reported that he had asked the rabbi and the governor for official permits allowing us to depart for Eretz Israel. They answered that without the permission of the British we could not leave Italy. This was a hard blow.

As compensation for the bad news, we received a letter

from Rabbi Zoller in Trieste. He had followed us with a paternal interest, asking how we were making out and what the prospects were. But a better and more concrete piece of encouragement came from our comrade Sapir. From Rome, 2,000 lire were coming for living expenses, and also an invitation to come to Rome where we would certainly succeed in getting the required permission to go further.

The few days we spent in Genoa were also utilized for sightseeing. We found the dead more interesting than the living. We went to *Camposanto*, the cemetery where Catholic, Protestant and Jewish bodies are buried. Never before in our lives did we see such opulence with so many statues, such elegant tombs built like miniature palaces. The Christian section was most attractive. There was distinct class structure, the poor segregated from the rich. The poor graves were neat and interestingly adorned, but the section inhabited by the rich was unbelievable. These were not ordinary graves topped by simple tombstones. They were fabulous mausoleums. In front of many of these mausoleums stood large statues, figures of saints and angels and bronze busts of the deceased. On many of the marble stones were engraved lines from Italian poets. It was not a cemetery but a museum filled with priceless artistic treasures.

In addition to the individual graves there were galleries where rows upon rows of stone containers held the remains of the deceased. The cemetery was of such gigantic dimensions that it would have taken days to see it all. Just as the Christian section was aristocratically wealthy, the Jewish sector was modestly impoverished; with the exception of a few well-to-do monuments, Jews had simple gravestones. Reading the inscriptions we learned some of the history of the Jews of Genoa. Most of the names were Italian and Spanish. But there were some of German-Ashkenazic origin, Polish and even Russian names. Nearly all the inscriptions were in Italian, but there were also some in the Holy Tongue.

An Italian Jew who guided us through *Camposanto*, told us in earnest that the cemetery was worth not less than the living city on the opposite side of the park.

We did not stay long. On January 22 the first group went to Rome. I went with the second group. Since the train departed in the morning, we stayed up in the station all night. All our adventures so far, the ups and downs, did not break our spirit, and our determination was not weakened one iota. When we boarded the Rome-bound train, our hearts were as joyous as when we had started off from Cracow for Vienna, from Vienna to Trieste, from Trieste to Genoa.

Now we were headed for the Italian capital where we had promises that we would certainly get permits to go forward. We sat at the windows, eagerly looking outward at the vistas, at the towns and villages and cities. The pleasant images passed swiftly by, and it wasn't long before the train entered the majestic Roman depot, the *Stacioni Termini*.

ROME

WE ARRIVED IN ROME ON JANUARY 24, WITH MIXED FEEL-
ings. First we believed that in the capital of Italy, where there
was a large Jewish community with many Jewish organizations, we would finally obtain legal permission to go to Eretz
Israel. Secondly, for us young Jewish students Rome had
another facet: the city was not only the capital of the ancient
Roman Empire but also a repository of untold historical treasures, of remains of antiquity and the later renaissance of art
and culture. Even more, Rome played an important part in
Jewish history. Jews had lived there without interruption for
over two thousand years. Jewish history had been a blend of
tremendous achievements and bitter persecution, of epochs
during which Roman Jews played a vital role in the scientific,
political and financial spheres. And there were periods when
the Jews were driven into the ghetto. Rome was the history
of popes, some of whom were friendly to the Jews and others
who hated us.

On the train we planned to cover all the Jewish and non-
Jewish art centers in the Eternal City. So we planned, until
the moment we arrived at the bustling station. But as in Trieste and Genoa, we experienced hot and cold. Rome taught
us the same lesson: not to have high expectations and not to
fall into deep depression. And to be patient. This time patience required that we accept a waiting period of not a day
not a week but two months.

When we entered the city, we contacted the Chief Rabbi, who told us an amazing fact: if we would agree to be considered internees by the Roman authorities, we would get free meals. We rejected this odd suggestion.

We registered in a hotel named "Albergo Paradiso." The word Paradiso implied that it was to be a Garden of Eden, but it was a poor hostel, lacking the amenities of paradise. Members of other *Halutz* units were also in the hotel, and we soon became one close-knit family.

We had to be prudent with our funds, and lived on two lire a day. Our staples were bread and water. Our smokers cut their cigarettes in two. From the first day we imposed strict discipline so that the group would not be penalized for the misbehavior of the few. We knew that the authorities had an eye on us. They were particularly concerned lest we be communists. One of our members did misbehave; we threatened him with a pistol, ordering him to leave us and go back to Poland, which he did.

When we realized that our departure was not imminent, our musician, Joseph Millet, organized a chorus and an orchestra so that we could entertain ourselves in the meantime. Our musical enthusiasm was so great that the hotel-keeper threatened to throw us out. We promised her to tone it down.

To save money, we slept two in a bed. When one member developed a skin ailment we all trooped to a hospital to be smeared with a special ointment, to protect us from the spread of the disease.

One day we sent a delegation to the Questura, the Ministry of Police, where we explained our situation. The Questura agreed to allot to each of us two lire daily on the account of the Russian government.

We did not cease our attempts to find an early way out, but the search dragged on and on without success. We had plenty of time to explore Rome.

Ceshek Rosenthal was elected planner and guide for our

tours. For weeks we went among the ancient ruins and the modern glories of Rome. First we went to the Roman Forum, to see the excavations that recalled the days when the Roman Empire ruled the world of antiquity. Here on remnants of palace walls, on crumbling columns of the grandiose government buildings, we scribbled curses against the new Polish regime which in its new-found independence launched pogroms against its Jewish citizens.

We went from ruin to ruin until we came upon the Arch of Titus, the triumphal gate of the Emperor whom we call Titus the Wicked, who had so brutally destroyed Jerusalem. On the Arch is a relief depicting the Jewish captives, locked in chains, laden with the treasures of the Holy Temple. The chief trophy taken by the Romans from the Temple was the seven-branched candlebrum. There is also a rendering of the sacrificial altar and the trumpets of the Temple. Standing by the Arch of Titus, I recalled that the Jewish captives refused to pass under it until they were lashed mercilessly, and some even died rather than submit to the ignominy. At the head of the parade marched Yohanan of Gush Halav and Simeon bar Giora.

We visited the Colosseum, the greatest historical remnant of ancient Romans, where the gladiatorial spectacles were held for the amusement of the populace. In this huge arena, Christians and others were devoured by lions, and gladiators fought to the death. The ruling classes of Rome attended, as did the Emperor and his entourage. Sitting in his loge, he would signal with his thumb whether the victorious gladiator should slay the vanquished or spare his life. The Caesars gave their people "bread and circuses," winning their affection and loyalty.

At the Colosseum I recalled the novel of the Nobel prize winner, Henrik Sienkiewicz, *Quo Vadis*, which depicted the martyrdom of the early Christians. We saw the iron gates through which the gladiators emerged into the arena, and the opposing gates through which the wild lions charged.

A poem by Y. L. Gordon surfaced in my memory, "Between Lion's Teeth." Gordon describes how two lovers, Marasa and Shimon, died, Shimon as a gladiator and Marasa who jumped into the arena so that she could perish together with her beloved. As we trod through the shattered ruins I imagined how I would have belonged among the thousands of Romans who had come to see this bloody sport and heard the shouting of the gladiators: *Ave imperatoria morituri te salutant*—those who are about to die salute you!

Early in our stay Ceshek took us to the Vatican, the fortress of Catholicism. The immense plaza spread out in front of St. Peter's was bounded on two sides by tall columns and religious statuary. The Basilica had been erected by master builders and architects, and inside were interred the remains of succeeding popes.

Inside the Vatican is the extraordinary Papal Museum, the Pinacoteca containing the Salon of Raphael—a priceless collection of paintings, sculpture, goblets, gold utensils embossed with precious stones. We saw the Sistine Chapel with the monumental frescoes and sculptures of Michelangelo, depicting stories from the Bible.

We also visited the Church of St. Peter in Chains. According to Christian lore, the Romans kept the early Christian missionaries here. A statue of Moses, by Michelangelo, stands in a niche. Moses has two horns projecting from his forehead, and he holds the Tablets in his arms. He looks so lifelike, with his veins and muscles so realistically carved in solid marble by that genius, Michelangelo. Moses seems about to rise and deliver a speech.

One day we visited the catacombs, underground tunnels where the first Christians held their illegal services, for they were persecuted by the pagan Romans. A multitude of graves, including graves of Jews, fills the catacombs. These graves are proof of the ancient history of the Jews of Rome. They are outside the city proper. By candlelight, one can make out the inscriptions and artwork on the catacomb walls. Walking through these tunnels, we thought with bitterness that these same Christians, who had been so persecuted for their religion in those days, were to become persecutors of others when they had seized power. We remembered how they were to burn Jews at the stake, and how Jews, like the early Christians, had to hide in order to meet for their daily prayers.

On January 31 we went to the ancient Roman ghetto. The streets were small, cramped, twisting, near the river Tiber; they were lined with small houses, stores and synagogues. We were the only ones there not dressed in Italian style, which caused many to stare at us.

An Italian Jew trailed us. To show that he was Jewish, he began to chant *Shma Yisrael*, and pointing to himself he said, "Yehudi." He pulled out from his shirt an amulet. We were sure that he was a tourist guide and we let him show us around. After a half hour, we wanted to pay him for his troubles, but he refused to accept our tips. He was insulted, as he was a volunteer who wanted to be hospitable, not out to make some money.

New groups of *Halutzim* continued to arrive in Rome. Some came singly. Most wanted to get to Eretz Israel, but some had given up hope that they would ever reach their goal after encountering so much hardship enroute from Poland to Rome. The latter decided to turn back to their home towns. In our Lodz group we had no such cases. We stuck together with a sense of determination.

The Jewish press wrote about us in many countries and in Rome the *Pro-Israelite* gave us a write-up. When we heard that a Zionist conference was to be held in London, we sent a telegram, in French, asking that they prevail upon the British to give us Palestinian visas.

Rabbi Dante Lattes, the noted leader of the Jewish community, was going to the London Zionist conference, and we gave him a letter addressed to the delegates, pleading for their assistance.

71

Some Russian political emigres also took an interest in our fate. Among them were Dr. Jacob Bluvstein and Dr. Moshe Beilinson. Dr. Beilinson was the tutor for a prominent Italian Jewish family which was close to the Italian government. We asked him to intervene on our behalf, to influence his friends, and he promised to do so. He was very interested in our group. He was an eye specialist who had come to Italy from Switzerland. He had become so fluent in Italian he could translate literary works from the Italian.

Steady reports of anti-Jewish excesses came from Poland, about the beating of Jews and throwing them off trains. We had a meeting with a Polish delegation then in Rome. One of them, an airforce pilot, told us that he was ashamed of the anti-Semitic behavior. He maintained that the excesses were not prompted by the Polish government but were inspired by unknown individuals.

On February 12 the famous Russian Zionist, Menachem Ussishkin, came to Rome, en route to the London conference. We went to hear him at the Great Synagogue. Later we tried to arrange for him to receive our representative, and on February 14 Jacob Skosovski did get to see him. Ussishkin was urged to do all in his power to facilitate our immediate departure for Eretz Israel.

But the reception by Ussishkin was an unexpected, bitter disappointment. He roared: "What kind of privileged characters are you? There are thousands of young people in Russia and Poland who want to go to Israel." This reaction was resented by us; we had not expected such a chilling reply from such a distinguished Zionist leader.

But every disappointment was followed by a hopeful piece of news. Our new-found friend, Dr. Beilinson, told us that his Italian friend had persuaded an Italian landowner to hire us to work on his estate, and on February 15 we went to work at Ponto Luciano, near Barka Tivoli. As soon as we arrived we were ushered into a farmhouse in which we were all to live. We each got a spade and early next morning we set to work. This gave us employment for the duration of our stay in Italy; secondly, more important, agriculture would give us the best experience for our future labors in Eretz Israel.

On February 17 we were sent to a swampy field where we were to gather up thin sticks and pile them in different parts of the field. We intended to become skilled farmers in Eretz Israel and this gave us a chance to become familiar with the menial art of piling up sticks! A mounted overseer supervised our work. He assigned us our tasks and saw to it that our performance was satisfactory.

One day, when we were in a light mood, we decided to stage a mock religious procession. We pulled our shirts out over our trousers and with shovels raised aloft like banners, we paraded around and sang *Hospodo Pomilu*, a song that Russians sang during their religious ceremonies. Our supervisor was bewildered and ordered us to halt the procession, but we gesticulated with our hands to let him know that this was a sacred ceremony and we paraded around the field several times. The following day we were given more work with shovels.

On a free day we trooped to neighboring Tivoli, where the Roman emperors had their summer villas. We visited the Villa Adriana and the magnificent gardens replete with statuary. We spent our evenings talking about our future in Israel. We sang a lot and lived in intimate friendship, like one big family.

We worked diligently, but it was slow, monotonous labor. We therefore asked our supervisor for some acreage where we could do piece work. We figured we could accomplish more in less time. He granted our request. From that day on, we worked faster and finished our assignment by noon. The afternoons were free and we could travel around the region.

One day, unexpectedly, three comrades arrived from Zgierz, Yoav Katz, Moshe Aharon Cooperman, and Kornstein, who had left home on January 15. We were very happy to see them and hear news about our families and friends.

On March 3 I went with Yoav Katz to Rome, where I posted a letter to my father in Canada. My friend Rubin wrote the letter in French, for censorship reasons. At that time we received a letter from Lodz, from Yusek Cohen, who was one of the scout leaders and was a good friend of mine, a student at the Jewish *gymnasium* in Lodz.

During our sojourn in Rome and now at our job in Ponto Luciano, we did not neglect for a minute our efforts to continue on our way to Eretz Israel. We had asked for free passage on a ship, and on March 9 we were informed that it had been granted. But the question remained: where do we find a ship?

News of the free trip made us drunk with joy, and a day later, we had an unexpected and welcome guest, Dr. Jacob Bluvstein, who had come to find out how we were doing. We took a group photo with him.

On March 11 Skosovski went to Rome to spur the matter of our departure, and on the same day Rabbi Dante Lattes returned from London with startling news that shook us up. Instead of helping us get permits from the British government, the leaders of the Zionist Conference advised us against going to Eretz Israel immediately. They maintained that immigration must be prepared properly and that in Eretz Israel facilities must be readied for absorbing the newcomers.

This report made us angry. We charged the Zionist leadership with shortsightedness. They did not understand the urgency, the need for swift realization of the dreams of *Aliyah*. Nor did they grasp the situation in which we found ourselves, that we were stranded midway, that we did not need cold, practical resolutions but actual, immediate help.

In addition there was another difficulty. The owner of the estate came to Barka Tivoli on March 12, and discovered that we were planning to leave. He dismissed us on the spot. We asked him to defer his decision and let us continue as before, as we simply had no place to stay in Rome. After pondering over it for a while, he gave in.

On March 15 Skosovski again went to Rome and this time returned with a brand new report: it had been decided that we should go to Naples, where we would be likelier to find a ship. Furthermore, the authorities had agreed to give us free railway tickets. Immediately we wrote two letters, a thank-you to the *Questura* for its friendly action and a second, public thank-you to the Italian newspapers.

On March 17 we again packed our goods and left Ponto Luciano for Rome. There we bade farewell to our two good friends, Dr. Bluvstein and Dr. Beilinson. We went to the depot in the evening, where we each got a lira and a half for pocket money. Since the train was leaving for Naples in the morning we spent the night at the station. It was not our first overnight stay in a railway depot, nor the first time that we were plagued all night by the thought: what will happen in Naples? Will the disappointments of Trieste, Genoa and Rome be repeated?

At dawn, the station began to fill up with people. Whistles blew and locomotives clanged, wheels clattered on the rails, and the loudspeakers blared announcements for the passengers waiting for their trian numbers.

Our train soon arrived, we boarded it and promptly at 10:48 a.m. it moved on. The wheels whirred along the rails and the rhythm began to affect our thoughts—what next? What next in Naples?

NAPLES

WE RENTED ROOMS IN A CHEAP HOTEL IN NAPLES. AFTER sleeping through the night, we arose bright and early to wind our way through narrow streets toward the port. It was raining and we got soaked as we forged along, asking directions from passersby. We found that a ship at anchor was to sail on March 24 for Alexandria, but the Naples police had not yet received word from Rome so there was no chance of our going.

We began our routine of searching for people who could help us. We began with a Zionist leader in Naples, a dentist named Dr. Vigdorchek, who was friendly and promised his assistance. Experience had taught us that promises were not enough and we had to work at it ourselves. We sent our comrade Sapir back to Rome, to exhort the *Questura* to send instructions to Naples.

Meanwhile the Naples police helped us in other ways: they gave each of us sixteen lire which helped us considerably, as our capital and food supplies were almost exhausted. On March 22 we heard that a telegram had come from Genoa with the news that we were to sail for Alexandria on March 26. This gave us a few more days for sightseeing.

People have different opinions about Naples. The most common view is that it is a beautiful city, that it is worth seeing—and dying. The other is that Naples is a singing city. Both views are correct. It is indeed beautiful and full of song.

All over town, even in the narrowest streets, lined with tall buildings and balconies, were carts and donkeys. With the merchants singing out their wares, it sounded like an opera.

Delighted and in a cheerful mood we strolled through the picturesque streets, entering museums, cathedrals and palaces, and the great San Carlo opera house. Around the city were mountain ranges bedecked with forests and on peaks were historic castles.

Above all we enjoyed the inhabitants of Naples who were very friendly. Whenever we had to inquire about the location of some site, a crowd assembled and everybody pitched in with answers, accompanied by lively gestures and broad smiles.

Mount Vesuvius rises behind the city. Two thousand years ago this volcano had erupted and destroyed Pompeii. We decided to visit this fire-spitting mountain. On March 23 we set out on foot and climbed up the broad sinewy terraces of frozen lava, until we reached the crater on top. We clambered around for hours, astonishment mingled with a bit of fear, as we studied the black precipice which stretched down into the bowels of the earth, from which a new wave of molten lava might come to create new ruins of mortal cities.

We visited Pompeii. The volcanic eruption had come so suddenly that many of the residents in their homes, the public buildings, the temples, and the recreation sites died instantly. Only 1,300 years later were layers of ashes removed and the city uncovered: the houses, the paved streets, the grandiose plazas. Human and animal bodies preserved by the hot lava were uncovered.

None of us dreamed that our innocent excursion would have severe consequences. Next day, Dr. Vigdorchek informed us that the chief of the *Questura*, who was a patient of his, told him in great detail about our tour of Vesuvius and that we had gone on the trip without notifying him in advance. He added that the chief of the *Questura* had told him that some of our members were dealing in foreign exchange.

He warned us that as long as we were in Naples we had to be careful.

A few days later we were shown how the *Questura* could be strict and pitiless. We had an opportunity to meet with members of other groups who had come a few weeks before from Rome without special permission. They were immediately interned by the secret police under harsh conditions. We could scarcely recognize them, they were so emaciated and in such an ugly mood. We were barely able to persuade the *Questura* to release them.

On March 28, Dr. Vigdorchek finally delivered the good news that we would get transportation the next day aboard a ship, and the next day, Spivak came running from the *Questura* with the order that we should pack our belongings!

Like small children, we jumped for joy. We took our baggage, rushed to the *Questura* headquarters and from there with happy steps walked to the port. There we stepped into a tender that took us to the larger vessel. It was not a luxury liner, but an old freighter. To us it was a floating palace.

Our newfound friend, Dr. Vigdorchek, accompanied us to the ship. We embraced him and thanked him heartily for his deep interest and practical help. We danced and sang and wound up with a lusty rendition of *Hatikva*.

Around two o'clock in the morning the ship lifted anchor and left the harbor for the wide sea. We were fed an evening meal of biscuits and cheese.

The decision to sail was so sudden that the ship's crew did not have time to prepare beds for us and we had to sleep on the floor. When we opened our eyes in the morning we were at sea. The waters were calm and overhead was a clear blue sky lit at the eastern end by the rising sun. We had breakfast of bread and coffee. At noon we had Italian macaroni, meat and bread; at night, the fare was again biscuits and coffee.

The placid sea was a pleasant contrast to the turbulent days and weeks of wandering on land, of riding on noisy trains. Our exalted mood was in sharp contrast to the earlier feelings of tension, of expectations denied and hopes delayed, of highs and lows when our spirits soared to heaven with delight and fell earthward with a jolt.

We sat all day on deck, and though we were surrounded by comrades, we each felt alone, isolated with his own quiet happiness, thoughts, longings. From time to time our joy surfaced, and we seated ourselves on deck, singing loudly all the Yiddish and Hebrew songs that we knew. English officers and soldiers were aboard ship and they looked at us with unfriendly eyes; we must have seemed outlandish to them, and we disturbed their rest.

We paid little attention to their stares and to the discomfort of sleeping on the hard floor with the valises tucked under our heads and the none too palatable meals. The ship was sailing forward and we knew that with each knot that we covered we were nearing the last stage of our wanderings.

On March 31 we reached Malta, where we took on coal. At 2 a.m. we weighed anchor again, and reached Alexandria on April 1. In Alexandria we met a group of comrades who had arrived before us and we joined them at their hotel.

Alexandria was a revelation. It is situated where the Nile meets the Mediterranean. We knew its history, that it is one of the oldest ports in the world and bears the name of Alexander the Great. Furthermore, it was one of the greatest commercial centers of the ancient world. Once there was also a mighty Jewish community and a flourishing Jewish culture. According to Josephus Flavius, Jews settled in Alexandria in the third century before the common era, and there were times when two-fifths of the residents were Jews. But as always, Jewish material and cultural prosperity did not endure for long. The Jews were oppressed by the Romans, and later by the Christians. There were times when Judaism flourished and times when it was repressed and the Jewish libraries and synagogues were set ablaze. But the Jews always came back. And now, as we docked at Alexandria, we met hosts of Jews.

We met Jews whose families had lived there for generations. There were also Jews who had come recently. We met transient American Jews who had served in the Jewish Legion during the war, and were returning home. There were also some Jewish servicemen from other countries who had come to Egypt on leave.

We spent several days waiting for permission to take the train to Palestine. Life around us was tumultous, a motley scene, a mixture of races and cultures. For the first time we confronted Egypt and its lifestyle. The city was filled with the remnants of previous cultures, of the ancient Greeks and Romans. We touched the Orient for the first time, the narrow streets and crowded bazaars and yelling peddlars, and the tiny coffee houses jammed with people.

We were absorbed by this new, strange, exotic scene. We visited the synagogue where we encountered all sorts of Jews. There was also a Zionist headquarters where we went to hold our meetings. On April 13 at the meeting hall of the Zeire Zion our members convened to discuss who would go ahead to Eretz Israel first. The decision was logical: the first should be those who had left Poland first.

The next day, the first group went on to Cairo. On April 15 it was our turn, those from Lodz and Zgierz. We took the train to Cairo, where we were met by the Zionist leader, Cheransky.

It was Passover eve and we had no time to scout around. We managed to check into a hotel and get ready quickly as we had been invited to a *Seder* at the Saloniki restaurant. It was a *Seder* night that I shall remember all my life. It was held in a brightly lit hall, tables covered with white cloths and around them were seated a fine assemblage of men and women who had come to welcome us. The *Seder* was conducted with jubilation and with all the traditional trimmings. We sang the songs of the *Haggadah*, followed by our own melodies. Late at night, rejuvenated, we returned to our hotel.

We had little time the next morning for sightseeing, but we did glimpse the pyramids from afar. The consciousness that we were spending Passover in Egypt made us even more aware of the significance of our surrounding. Our pending departure seemed to be a reenactment of the Biblical drama.

The next morning, we entrained for Eretz Israel. It was a never-to-be-forgotten day, not simply because it was our own Exodus from Egypt but primarily because on that morning a unique personal drama unfolded.

We were to get up very early, and since I always had trouble rising, a defect which has abided with me to this day, I asked a comrade to waken me. But in the hustle and bustle he forgot to do so. When I opened my eyes I wondered why it was so quiet. I dressed quickly and ran around the hotel rooms. They were silent, empty. It dawned on me what had happened. In panic I grabbed my baggage and ran into the street, stopped the first cab, but the Arab driver didn't know where I wanted to go. I tried all kinds of signals, whistling like a locomotive, but he couldn't understand me. Luckily a man passing by saw my predicament and after inquiring about my troubles, told the cabby to take me to the railway. The Arab whipped up his horse, but we got to the station too late. The train had left.

Desperate, I went to the ticket office to purchase a ticket for the next train, but I was told that I needed a permit, which I did not have, since our group had a collective ticket and pass.

I was at a loss. What to do? I waited until another group of comrades arrived from Cairo and boarded the train with them, sitting next to a British officer. When the conductor came to check the tickets, the officer knew my dilemma, that I did not have a ticket, and he told the conductor that I was with him and to let me alone.

At one o'clock the train arrived at Kantara. Here I was completely lost, not knowing what would happen next. But things had been straightened out for me by Skosovski, who had ridden with the first group. He saw that I was missing and showed the railway officials our group ticket, stressing my name and the fact that I was coming on a later train. Now the officials asked for my name and credentials to prove my identity and seeing that I was the tardy passenger, allowed me to cross the border.

I keep referring to a "train" but it was really a small chain of open coaches pulled by an old French locomotive. Among the passengers on the train was the famous writer and idealist who had done so much to revive the Hebrew language, Eliezer Ben Yehuda. He and his wife had come to settle in Eretz Israel back in 1881, a year before the first *Biluim*. His aim was to transform the Holy tongue into a living language. It has been told that when he and his wife were sailing from Marseilles to Jaffa, he told her that henceforth they would speak only Hebrew. They settled in Jerusalem. When their first son was born a year later, they did not allow anyone near him who did not speak Hebrew. Ben Yehuda, whose former name had been Perlman, was the one who decided that Hebrew should be spoken with the Sephardic accent. The father of modern Hebrew, Ben Yehuda compiled a dictionary, even coining the Hebrew word for dictionary, *milon*. He sat with us in the open coach and talked with us all the time.

On April 19, 1919, we reached Lod. We had left Lodz on December 3, 1918, some four and a half months earlier. After this long, arduous journey we finally stepped onto the soil of Eretz Israel. We were the first harbingers of the Third *Aliya*.

THE FIRST DAYS

WE FOLLOWED THE SEASHORE FOR A LONG TIME UNTIL WE came to the first stop, El Arish. As we proceeded, we saw the sea to the left and endless desert to the right. We stopped only a few minutes in Gaza where the train swerved to the east in the direction of Lod. From then on we saw only wilderness, tracts of land dotted with cliffs and rocks, sand and waste. Occasionally we saw bits of cultivation, land covered with a green carpet and trees. From time to time we saw the tiny clay houses of an Arab village.

This was all strange-familiar to us. I looked around at my comrades, who like myself were staring at the landscape and like myself were experiencing the sensation that everything around us, which was so exotic and strange, was at the same time homey and our own. We all felt that we had not come to a foreign country but to a land of kinship intimately ours. We had not just *arrived* but had *returned* home.

When the train halted at the small, primitive Lod station, our group was awaiting us under the leadership of Skosovski. There was also a delegation of *Hapoel Hatzair* headed by Zvi Lieberman. They greeted us heartily and took us to the office of the organization in Tel Aviv. When we dropped our luggage, Lieberman told us they would first of all help us find work. Zelig Reichert asked for permission to go to Degania where his teacher from Zgierz, Manoah, was, and he was allowed to go. Lieberman told us that there were jobs in Hadera and in Gan Shmuel. In the

83

colony of Hadera, Russian Jews had purchased some land where their company planted orange and olive trees. The owners had remained in Russia and the operations were run by their administrators. Those Jews had a two-fold purpose: to invest their money for profit, and to help in the development of the country. The *Kvutza,* Gan Shmuel, was nearby.

When Zvi Lieberman suggested that we seek work there, he warned that there was a lot of malaria in the area, and that only volunteers should go. Three of us responded quickly: Stark, Spivak and myself. That same afternoon horses were hitched to a wagon and we set off for Hadera. Jumping off the wagon at Hadera, we went to the workers' hostel, and we slept there overnight. This was our first night in the Land of Israel.

Next morning I went to work at the *Agudat Netaim* citrus grove. Like the other workers, Jews and Arabs, I got a maader, a hoe. The job was to dig irrigation channels around the orange trees. I was assigned to work alongside a Yemenite Jew named Zecharia. It was my first contact with a Yemenite and I learned a lot about this tribe of our people who had come to our homeland in the face of tremendous hardships. Individual Yemenites had come to the Land of Israel back in the 15th century but the real migration began after the Turks conquered Yemen and a path was opened for them, a hard path but at least it was open. The Jews left Yemen because of the persecution they suffered at the hands of their Moslem neighbors; but they came mainly because of *Hibat Zion*, the love of Zion, their ageless dream to return to Jerusalem. Many of them did settle in Jerusalem, where the majority of the Old *Yishuv* lived. Part of the community, mainly Jews from Eastern Europe, came to die in the Holy Land and they lived on *Halluka* charity.

Many of the Yemenites were craftsmen, including goldsmiths, silversmiths, engravers, shoemakers and building workers, who preferred hard work to living on charity. They spread out over the country and worked in the settlements. Zecharia was one of them. He worked skillfully and diligently with a hoe. He told me on one occasion that he was married, not just with one wife but with several, and with a gaggle of children.

We were under the supervision of a Jewish foreman who rode around on a horse, directing our work. When it was nearly time to stop working at a given hour, I noticed the foreman setting his watch. At quitting time, I turned to my Yemenite friend: "Zecharia, put down your hoe." He obeyed me, whereupon the foreman came charging up on his horse and asked why we had put aside our tools. I showed him that my watch indicated that the day of toil was over, but he pointed to his watch, showing that there was yet time for labor. I then told him that I had seen him turn his watch back. He became furious and yelled at me, "Bolshevik!" and fired me on the spot.

That was how my first day of work in the Land of Israel ended. However, I was not at all dismayed. I slept at the *Bet Hapoalim* and went to work the next day at **Gan Shmuel**, which I reached on foot.

Gan Shmuel was founded in 1896 by the Odessa Lovers of Zion Committee and was named in honor of a beloved leader of *Hovevei Zion*, Rabbi Shmuel Mohiliver. The settlement had 56 dunam planted with orange trees and citrons, with an additional 70 dunam in olive trees.

In 1906, the orchard was transferred to the Jewish National Fund and was worked by the *Yitzhar* company without success. In 1913 the Palestine Bureau attempted to convert the settlement into a collective *kvutza*, an independent commune, and gave the land to a group who would cultivate it independently. This was the first experiment to create a *kvutza* in Judea and Samaria (Degania had already been established in Galilee). Because of the prevailing malaria and the frequent illnesses (there were also several deaths) there was a steady turnover of people. The settlement was also the target of Arab attacks.

During the first World War, some members of Gan Shmuel were arrested by the Turks on suspicion of espionage. Others were drafted to chop down trees for military purposes. During the war years, Jewish refugees came from Judea to Hadera and Gan Shmuel because they were expelled from there by the Turks. The victims of malaria increased in number.

When I arrived, Gan Shmuel was a poor *kvutza*, with no more than thirty souls. Since Gan Shmuel was based on its groves, the economic condition was severe in the immediate post-war days, as there was no foreign market for oranges. But the trees had to be tended nevertheless. When I reported for work, they gave me, as they did to all, a hoe, and I set about fixing the soil around the trees. It was not easy labor as the clay soil became hard as a rock under the searing sun. It did not take long for my hands to swell and break out in blisters. The other workers watched me sweat it out. I was not only the newest but the youngest member of the crew. I exerted myself to the limit so that they would not guess how much this labor was costing me in pain. My hands ached, but I stubbornly worked on. So ended my first day at Gan Shmuel.

A small patch of grain was sown for the *kvutza's* own use. The grain was threshed in a primitive fashion, as the Arabs had been doing for centuries. A few planks were simply nailed together in the width, some holes were drilled below into which stones were fitted. The grain was spread out in a wide circle. A mule was harnessed to the board, which revolved over the grain. The eyes of the mule were covered so that it would not get dizzy. I trod around on the boards all day in a circle. It was boring, so I began to sing in Polish, Hebrew and Yiddish. The *kvutza* children jumped up on the board and rode along with me, which relieved the monotony somewhat.

In the *kvutza* was a concept that a newcomer had to be

initiated, so that he would experience all the happenings that they had experienced. Several times they said to me, "Look at the greenhorn! He wants comforts. Do you know how we worked? What we went through?" I compressed my lips and made no reply to their taunts.

There was a tradition that the comrade working with the horses was always in charge of them. I became close friends with Gershon Hanoch, who was to become a noted Hebrew writer. One Saturday evening, an agronomist was scheduled to speak at neighboring Hadera. We decided to attend the lecture. On the road between Gan Shmuel and Hadera was a small stream spanned by a small bridge. A plank was broken in the bridge. I was at this period in charge of the horses. The comrades were afraid that because of my inexperience I would not be able to handle the situation and they wanted to relieve me of my mules. But my friend Gershon whispered to me, "Don't let them. You are the boss. You have to drive the wagon." So I replied in that vein. The comrades were perplexed: "He has no experience. He will kill us all." I answered, "I am boss of the mules and I will drive the wagon. If you are afraid, go on foot." When we reached the bridge, they all hopped off the wagon and I proceeded to cross to the other side. This little incident raised my standing in the *kvutza*.

Another time I was not so lucky. We had to haul in the grain from the fields and the wagon tipped over. I was sure that the comrades would scoff at me, but just the opposite happened. They were good to me and said, "Don't feel bad. Now you are a real *baal agoleh*, a wagoner, because we have all had such an experience."

Work in the *kvutza* was hard, but I got accustomed to it, and became part of the daily life of the group. I belonged to the society. Days we spent at work, but evenings we spent on social activities and interminable discussions. There were already two party clusters in the *kvutza*, *Hapoel Hatzair* and *Ahdut Haavoda*, which had been organized recently. The debates focused on issues which related to us, the development of the land and the work.

Among the comrades was a Roumanian, Feldman, a well-built, athletic man. He was assigned the task of defense and security in the *kvutza*. One evening he proposed that I join him on a secret, dangerous mission. Not far from the railway station near Gan Shmuel, there were stores of German weapons and ammunition captured by the British from the Turks. Under cover of night, Feldman and I crawled on our stomachs to the station. The British guards were unaware of our presence, and we succeeded in getting hold of some guns and bullets which we added to the arsenal, such as it was, in Gan Shmuel.

I read every free minute. I became acquainted with the articles of A. D. Gordon, "Our Accounting with Ourselves," published in *Hapoel Hatzair*. They dealt with ideological questions and had a tremendous impact on my thinking. Gordon's visage was a striking one. He came from the Ukraine in 1904 at the age of forty-eight. There he worked as a bookkeeper for his relative, Baron Guinzberg. Back in 1898 he had written a strong polemic against Simon Dubnow, the celebrated Jewish historian, who was advocating the concept of Diaspora Nationalism. Gordon argued that "Zionism is not a mystic messianism but a healthy idea for the revival of the Jewish people in its own land through a life of creativity and labor."

Gordon devoted much time to the education of youth. His home was a gathering place for young people. Every Saturday evening they would come to hear his lectures and listen to his discourses on the national rebirth of the Jews and about the land of Israel. He founded a modern school for boys and girls, where they learned Hebrew and other subjects. In his conversations, he waxed enthusiastic about the renewal of the Jew through agricultural work in Israel.

Gordon did not talk in abstractions. He decided to be a

personal example. Before coming to Eretz Israel he had never done any manual labor, yet he was convinced that the rebirth of the Jews was impossible without a life of creation and a life of work. He was offered a post as teacher and librarian, but he refused this employment. Gordon went to Petah Tikva where he finally got a job on an orange plantation. He was overjoyed. In a letter to his family, he wrote: "Can you imagine that your father has become a simple laborer? I feel as though I have been newly born."

Despite his lack of experience in manual labor and his advanced age, Gordon rejected the attempts of his younger colleagues to ease his lot. On the contrary, he encouraged others to overcome the hardship and to adjust to the primitive life. At meetings of workers, Gordon would stir up his listeners, not to bow their heads, not to shame the manhood in themselves, and not to relinquish their dignity for the sake of self interest or comfort. Especially, he stressed that they should stand up for the idea of Jewish national freedom and redemption. With his profound thoughts on the vital importance of labor, on the relation of man to nature, on justice and righteousness, Gordon became a symbol for the Jewish workers in the land of Israel and for the Jewish youth in the diaspora. I read his essays avidly. They provided encouragement and strengthened my yearning to follow in his footsteps.

Meanwhile, I had not chosen to belong to any political party. The newcomers, most of whom belonged to *Hashomer Hatzair*, had decided to organize a separate unit. However a few of us maintained that upon our arrival in the country we should not isolate ourselves but join one of the existing groupings.

The *Ahdut Haavoda* earnestly tried to enroll the newcomers in Gan Shmuel. They sent one of their outstanding leaders to talk to us, David Remez. Together with Berl Katznelson, Shmuel Yavnieli and others, he had founded *Ahdut Haavoda* (Unity of Labor). In later years Remez was to become secretary-general of Histadrut, the labor federation, and Israel's first Minister of Transportation.

Remez delivered an incisive speech, to which I listened carefully. I, who had been under the strong influence of A. D. Gordon, posed many questions which Remez answered patiently and to the point. But in the end he did not convince me, and I decided to affiliate with *Hapoel Hatzair*.

The material conditions in the *kvutza* were difficult. Since we could not sell our oranges, we had to find work elsewhere. Some of us went to work in the vineyard of Dr. Hillel Jaffe near Zichron Yaakov. Dr. Jaffe maintained the principle of Jewish labor, and I shall return to this matter again. I just want to state here that in those days there were Jewish colonists, landowners, who did not hire Jewish workers. They did this for several reasons. Arab hands were cheaper. Secondly, Arabs were accustomed to farm work and the Jewish landowners were convinced that they worked better. There were also colonists who resented the Jewish workers for not being pious and that many were imbued with East European ideas of socialism.

Dr. Hillel Jaffe was an exception who did employ Jews. We went to work in his vineyards each morning taking along a bag with a few dozen oranges which would quench our thirst during the day as water was very scarce. I worked alongside a comrade named Fishman. I think he was related to Rabbi Fishman and Ada Fishman. Usually he was a quiet one, but during rest breaks he would tell me about his life and how he had come here. He was bitter about the attitude of the Jewish colonists. I heard this complaint from many sources, and I was soon to witness it myself.

An incident occurred that opened for me a new aspect of Jewish life in the land of Israel at that time: the Arab question. During my first hours in the country I saw the Arabs at El Arish, in Gaza, and then in Lod. But in those first days it was not a subject to give me much thought. In Lodz and Zgierz we ignored the question of the Arabs in Palestine. All we knew was that we were returning to our historic homeland and we rarely thought about the Arab population. But the longer I was in the land of Israel, the more did I realize that it was not a simple matter.

An adjacent Arab village was not friendly to us and we had little contact with it. One day a fire broke out in the Arab village. As we saw the flames, we rushed with water pails to extinguish them. We concentrated on the area where grain was stored and we succeeded in saving part of it.

I was astonished, however, to find that instead of being happy, the Arabs cried out bitterly. When we told them they ought to be happy that they were not completely burned out, some of them, in tears, let us know that it was not their land, that it belonged to an absentee sheikh who took most of the produce. Since some of the grain was burned, they would now have to pay for it and they would be enslaved to the sheikh for a long time to come. This incident taught me something about the social situation of the Arab peasants, which also affected their relations to the Jews.

As I have already mentioned, when we arrived in the country, representatives of *Hapoel Hatzair* warned us that there was malaria in Gan Shmuel. So we discovered. To fight off the fever, we were given quinine. The quinine was wrapped in cigarette paper in the form of pills. I showed resistance to the disease and did not catch malaria; hence I was appointed to distribute the quinine among the sick.

IN PETACH TIKVA

BEFORE LEAVING LODZ, I WAS ASKED BY MY MOTHER AND other family members to call on a relative living in Petach Tikva. His name was Baruch Golomb. One free day I visited Petach Tikva, not only to visit my relative but to see this first Jewish settlement in the renewed Israel. Petach Tikva had been founded in 1878 by Jews from the Old *Yishuv* in Jerusalem. It was the "Mother of the Settlements"—*Em Hamoshavot*. The settlers did their own work and only later did they begin to hire Arabs. When the Second *Aliya* began they did not want to employ the new wave of pioneers; Arabs worked for less money, and the landowners libelled the young Jewish hands, saying that they were too weak and not as productive as the Arabs.

Kibbush Ha'avoda, the conquest of work, was the slogan of the young Jewish pioneers who made a superhuman effort to prove their worth as agricultural workers. These inexperienced youths began to compete with the more primitive but experienced Arab workers. Many grew weak, or fell sick. Some who could not endure the ordeal left the country, but the remainder waged the struggle for *kibbush ha'avoda* in spite of the frequently inhuman attitude of the Jewish employers. They didn't earn enough for food and clothing but they did not surrender. Some landowners tried to get rid of the Jewish workers. They insulted and belittled them, but the young pioneers suffered all the indignities for the sake of a day's work.

In Petach Tikva, as in the other colonies, at the time of hiring seasonal workers, it was customary to line up all the applicants, Jews and Arabs, in the market place, where the landowners examined them and felt their muscles. They usually picked the Arabs and let the Jews stand there without saying a word. When a Jew was selected, and he reported for work in a grove, the Arabs rushed ahead to pick out the best hoes and left the worst for the Jews. Sometimes the Arabs bullied the Jews and spitefully speeded up their work. The Jews did their best to keep up but they tired first and lost their energy. But they did not fall out, and continued to work. After some time, the Jews gained experience in the orange and olive groves and in the vineyards. Yet, the relationship between the Jewish colonists and the Jewish workers in Petach Tikva was filled with animosity.

Another reason for the tension was that the Jews were not as servile as the Arabs. Furthermore, the Jewish workers had spiritual needs; they organized cultural events and lectures which were attended by the children of the colonists. The fathers were not happy that their offspring mingled with the *shmendriks*. A third reason was religious fanaticism. The colonists were angry that the young workers did not go to the synagogue on the Sabbath.

When pogroms struck the Jews of Russia during the revolution of 1905, the workers in Petach Tikva decided to hold a memorial meeting. On the program was a recitation of Bialik's poem, *Al Hashchita* (On the Massacre). The colonists strongly opposed the meeting, complaining: "There are pogroms in Russia and you stage meetings?" The workers replied that the victims were their own parents, their families, and that their pain was greater than that of the colonists, but nothing helped. The meeting was to have been held in the home of Gissin, but the colonists threatened that if he allowed it he would be fined.

93

The workers decided to hold the meeting in a smaller home, for themselves. When they finished work and began to prepare for the meeting, they found Arabs standing at the door who did not let anyone in. They had been sent by the Jewish landowners. Our young men drove the Arabs away and the meeting was held. Next day the landowners' committee decided that the Jewish workers must leave Petach Tikva forthwith. When the workers did not obey, the employers ordered no one to hire them.

Some workers were driven out of their lodgings. The colonists declared that the boycott would not apply to those workers who would sign a statement that they would conform to the committee's demands: they would attend synagogue services every Sabbath and festival; they would not carry canes on the Sabbath; they would not walk outside the Sabbath pale; and they would not attend any event without the consent of the committee. Understandably, no one signed. The result was that seventy men were unemployed, many of them on the verge of starvation. Comrades from other places sent aid, and the question of quitting Petach Tikva altogether was raised. Aaron David Gordon encouraged the workers and urged them not to leave.

The colonists did not cease their persecution. Some time passed, and the Arabs, together with representatives of the landowners, broke into the workers' library, which was located in a doctor's house. They pulled out the books and the shelves. The Jewish workers sank into an even deeper depression. One by one, they began to leave Petach Tikva.

This happened in 1906. Now, fourteen years later I went to call on my relative, a Jewish colonist! He had his own *Pardes*, orange grove, and he was also the supervisor of other groves which belonged to some Jews in Lodz. As I entered Petach Tikva, I saw before me a beautiful settlement with a broad main street flanked by nice homes with lawns and gardens. Orange trees were planted all around, and further afield were grains and vegetables.

My relative was glad to see me. He welcomed me into his home and served refreshments. Then he proudly showed me his possessions. We both rode off on donkeys to see the groves outside the town. There was much activity in the field, but among the workers I did not see a single Jew. All were Arabs. I rode silently, although there was so much I wanted to say.

When we returned to the house, I met his two children, a boy and a girl. I found out that there was no peace between the children and their father. The son and daughter had rebelled against him because he would not hire Jewish workers, and they went to work in a neighboring settlement, Be'er Tuvia. They had come home for a visit.

In the house I began a discussion. How did he, a Jewish landowner in the land of Israel, not employ any of the young Jewish idealists who had come to build the land? He answered crudely that Jews were not fit for hard labor like the experienced Arab peasants. In a rage, I asked him bluntly: "What would happen if I, your relative, was in dire circumstances, starving, would you give me a job?"

He sprang up in anger and replied hypocritically: "I should allow a Rosenblum grandson to work like an Arab? Never in your life!" Now I understood why his two children were so angry, why they didn't want to live in his house and went elsewhere.

It was a painful episode but it revealed to me the problem of the relations between the Jewish landowners and the young *Halutzim*. I comprehended the meaning of the struggle, of *kibbush ha'avoda*, a campaign in which I was to become actively involved.

CONFERENCE IN KINNERET

AFTER PASSOVER I BEGAN TO WORK IN GAN SHMUEL. DUR-
ing Shavuot an important agricultural conference of *Hapoel
Hatzair* was held at the Kinneret settlement on the shores of
the Sea of Galilee. *Hapoel Hatzair*'s followed on the heels of
another agricultural conference held at Petach Tikva under
the aegis of *Achdut Ha'avoda*.

For me it was to be an extraordinary event. Two delegates
were sent by Gan Shmuel, Shabtai Nutkin and myself. I was
to be the representative of the new immigrants. At the conference I met for the first time comrades from various settlements in all parts of the country, including outstanding personalities whose names I knew but whom I had not yet seen
in person. I heard reports from representatives of new settlements, and the latest facts and figures about the new *Yishuv*,
which gave me a deeper insight into the achievements and
problems that faced us, the builders of the land. I listened in-
tensely to the debates, which were not theoretical exercises
but dealt with living, practical issues.

Nutkin and I went to Kinneret in a wagon pulled by two
horses. We drove through Samarian hills to the valley of Jez-
reel. It was a drab road, on both sides of which stretched
empty acres of untilled soil. There was no sign of a living
settlement. Our first stop was at Merhavia, founded in July

96

1911 by the colonization society of the Zionist Organization. Based on plans of Professor Franz Oppenheimer, it introduced the first cooperative form of economy.

From Merhavia we proceeded to Yavniel, one of the first Jewish settlements in the country, founded in 1901. The settlers worked on their own land. Then we continued to Kinneret.

From the distance we saw a lovely tree-lined settlement, where the Jordan River flows from Lake Kinneret, the Sea of Galilee. Kinneret was founded in 1908 with the backing of the Palestine Bureau of the World Zionist Organization. In 1912, an American group, *Haikar Haoved*, founded a *kvutza* on the site. The leader was Eliezer Yaffe, who had studied agronomy in America. Together with an earlier group of workers, the Americans took over operations.

The Americans were very capable and in the first year the deficit shrank in comparison with previous years. The group appealed to their friends in America to come and join the *kvutza*, but nobody responded and the disappointed American comrades left the place at the end of the summer. One returned to the United States, another went to Ben Shemen, and another to Milhamia. Only Yaffe decided to remain and organize some Israelis to stay at Kinneret. He suggested to the Palestine Office that the group should undertake to work on its own responsibility, but nothing came of his plan. Finally, the Palestine Bureau invited a group from Kfar Uriah to come to Kinneret. In the course of time, many celebrated personalities were to live at Kinneret, one of them being Berl Katznelson.

When we arrived we found quite a few already assembled for the conference. Yaacov Zaslavsky (Uri) and Natan Hofshi came from Hulda; D. Giladi from Kfar Uriah; Zaslavsky from Be'er Tuvia; D. Rikovsky from Karkur; Shoshanno Rechthand-Yaffe from Mikveh Israel. Yael Gordon represented the women of Merhavia, and there were also delegates from Kinneret, Degania and Gan Shmuel.

The two central questions on the agenda were: *kvutza* (collective settlement or commune) and *moshav ovdim* (smallholders' settlement on a cooperative basis).

The external appearance of the delegates impressed me considerably. They were not dressed up in holiday clothes, such as was the custom in Poland at important gatherings, but simply in their work togs. We sat at simple tables, on benches. Nearly all the delegates were strangers to me, but some names rang a bell. There was Aaron David Gordon, dubbed "The Old Man." There was Joseph Bussel, famed for organizing the agricultural union in Galilee and a convenor of the conference. There was also Ada Fishman, who had a relative in our *kvutza* at Gan Shmuel. I think I was the youngest delegate.

After the reports on the condition of the settlements in the post-war era, Bussel delivered a long speech. A founder of Degania, he was the theoretician and defender of the idea of the *kvutza*. He spoke of the role of the *kvutza*, its development and its problems, which are related to the two goals of *kibbush hakarka* (conquest of the soil) and *kibbush ha'avoda* (conquest of work). He also spoke on how to achieve a society based on social justice.

Bussel's talk gave me new insight into the concept of the *kvutza*, of which I had only superficial knowledge before. Some of his phrases are indelibly written in my mind: "The *kvutza* was created by life; we wished to create life, a new life, to work by ourselves and be the defenders of our homes, and be the regulators of our economy, our cultural life and our social affairs. . . . There are those who seek new forms like the *moshav ovdim*. . . . I maintain that we have not yet finished the first experiment and we should not start a second one yet. . . ."

A discussion ensued, the problems were analyzed and solutions were bandied back and forth. There was a report on the girls' farm school at Kinneret that had been established two years earlier, in 1918. It was the first female commune in the country. Their representatives reported that they had started with vegetables and the market was a good one: the military had purchased the produce. That year ended with a profit but this year there was no local market, and because of the difficulty of transportation, the vegetables could not be shipped far away. Much of the crop was left to rot in the fields. Their new program was to introduce mixed farming, and they would buy livestock and chickens.

Bussel took the floor a second time, to stress the fact that the goal of the *kvutza* is self-labor, that the work had to be done by the members and not by hired hands. Only at the height of the harvest season did it happen (he was speaking of Degania) that hired workers were employed. Finally a solution was found: the hired workers were treated as *kvutza* members, receiving all the rights and the same wages and a share of the profits of the settlement, just like regular members.

In conclusion, Bussel stated: "We have introduced new work forms, we have increased the yield and this has given us strength and satisfaction. Our life was harsh; in the beginning we lived in tents. We hoped that when we constructed houses it would be easier to institute changes in our intimate society. When we moved into our houses, it was truly easier, but the health situation remained bad as before. We had too much land to cultivate, people came and went. . ."

Joseph Bussel also discussed women in the collective society. He said that the women had a hard life: "We have sinned against our women comrades. At least, men work outdoors in the field during the day, but they are tied to the house. Exceptionally difficult problems have arisen with the formation of the first family. The problem of child rearing has come to the fore. What is the role of women to be in this area? Are women suited to share in the management of the general economy, like men? We, therefore, decided (in Degania) that men should participate in domestic chores just like the women, both in the kitchen and in the house."

He concluded that the work was expanding, both in scope and in diversity, while the comrades were being overstrained by the harsh climate and by disease. "We therefore had to sacrifice diversification and try to reduce the deficit. During the war, we farmed large stretches of land in order to produce food for the entire *Yishuv*. Now, however, after the war, we have begun to retrench in order to work only enough acreage to meet our own needs with our own manpower. This year we are working only half our land, and even now we have to use some hired labor, because there are days when ten or fifteen comrades are on the sick list. We are going to try a new experiment next year: a number of families will work just enough land to support our home needs; other necessities will be provided by income from the dairy surplus and other farm branches whose yield will be marketed."

Aaron David Gordon took the floor, recalling that there were times when Degania's members suffered hardships, but they felt good: "Now, as I see the birthpangs of creation, I bless you and say to you: be happy that you have achieved what you have. This is the way."

During an intermission, Gordon surprised me by inviting me for a walk. We strolled along a road leading from Kinneret to Tiberias. He asked me about my family, my education, about the Jewish youth in Poland. What drove me and others to come to the land of Israel? What did we expect here? I felt a paternal interest in his conversation, and I was happy that Gordon had chosen me to walk by his side. He wanted to learn about the youth in the Diaspora. Could we expect a large influx of *Halutzim*?

I told him about our youth movement, how we had added the study of Hebrew to our program, as well as Palestine geography and life in the country. I told him of the dreams of many young people in the towns and cities of Poland to come to the land of Israel, of the training farms where they prepared for a life on the soil.

When we returned to the meeting hall, it was evening, the

eve of Shavuot. Ada Fishman, secretary of the conference, put down her pen and asked someone else to write the minutes since she did not write on Sabbath or holidays.

We recessed for the evening and the delegates went to Degania for a party to celebrate the arrival of a son. The proud parents were Miriam and Joseph Baratz. Since Joseph was in Russia at the time, on a mission to organize *Aliya,* we came to share the joy with the young mother, Miriam.

En route we had to ford the Jordan river, as there was no bridge. Some waded across in hip-deep water. Others went by wagon, but it was half submerged in the water and the passengers had to lift their feet into the air to avoid getting wet.

The history of Degania, the first *kvutza*, is linked with the story of an extraordinary person, Dr. Arthur Ruppin. Born in Germany, he studied at the University of Berlin, where he earned his doctorate as an economist and statistician. In Germany he edited a journal on Jewish demography and statistics. His aide was Dr. Jacob Thon, a young Zionist who had a strong influence on Ruppin. Dr. Ruppin participated in the seventh World Zionist Congress. Dr. Thon was eager for Ruppin to visit Palestine. He induced Otto Warburg, the Chairman of the Palestine Commission of the Zionist Action Committee to ask Ruppin to go to Palestine to survey the settlement possibilities.

Dr. Ruppin came to Eretz Israel in 1907 and stayed five months. He wrote a memorandum to the Zionist Action Committee, proposing that land be purchased in Galilee and Judea, where the largest Jewish communities were located and the nuclei of new settlements should be implanted. In April 1908, at Ruppin's initiative, the Zionist Organization founded the Palestine Land Development Company, based in Jaffa. Among the first projects of the Palestine Bureau was the planting of the Herzl Forest in Ben Shemen.

Dr. Ruppin, seeing that the Jewish landowners tended to hire Arabs, suggested that the new Jewish arrivals be taken directly into an agricultural economy which would be backed by Jewish societies on land of the Jewish National Fund. The Jewish workers would get half their wages from the society and earn the other half by their labor. On the eve of Shavuot, 1908, the first national farm was established near the Sea of Galilee, and it was called Kinneret.

Life was hard in the desolate spot. The heat was unbearable and almost all the settlers suffered from malaria. Food was bad. Nevertheless, the pioneers worked devotedly from morning to night, feeling that they were writing a new chapter in Jewish history and in the annals of the Jewish worker.

Kinneret invited Sarah Malkin, then in Sedjera, to join it and direct the household work. Grain, potatoes, and beans were planted on 2,500 dunam, over 600 acres. Because of a conflict between the workers and the agronomist in charge, a Mr. Berman, Dr. Ruppin came to Kinneret. In 1910, the farm was divided into two. The section known as Um Juni was taken over by a group of experienced workers from Hadera, who renamed the place Degania, the cornflower, the first commune. Joseph Bussel was among the founders, as were Joseph and Miriam Baratz.

We congratulated Miriam Baratz and tasted the refreshments, danced and sang song after song. Aging Gordon danced with abandon along with the youngsters, and I was drawn into the festivities, one of the most exalted moments of my life in Israel.

Next morning we returned to Kinneret to resume the conference. The discussion turned to the topic of the new settlement form, the *moshav ovdim*, with Zvi Yehuda as protagonist. He said it was no longer a theoretical matter, as the country was preparing to receive large numbers of immigrants. The question was: could the *Yishuv* afford to experiment with new forms of colonization or should it concentrate on helping newcomers to find work? Zvi Yehuda declared that neither had to suffer. Those who preferred a *moshav* should organize and elect people to deal with the practical aspects.

Preparatory work had to be done immediately. Rocks had to be cleared from the fields, swamps had to be drained, saplings had to be planted and plots had to be allocated. Yehuda's flaming oratory inspired us. Delegates rose to endorse his views. Among the resolutions adopted was one to establish a *kupat holim*, a health cooperative, for the agricultural workers who were members of *Hapoel Hatzair*.

The conference impressed me immensely. For the first time I saw how words were not mere words, but were convertible into action. Opinions were based on daily realities. I got a vivid picture of an evolving *Yishuv*, its difficulties and its hopes, its pains and its triumphs. I was happy to be a partner in this collective act of creation.

The conference was also a turning point in my personal life. I no longer felt like a greenhorn, and I returned to Gan Shmuel refreshed. From that day, I worked with even more persistence, disregarding the harsh weather, the broiling sun and the exhausting labor.

WHAT THE YISHUV LOOKED LIKE

DAYS AND WEEKS PASSED, DAYS OF SWEAT AND TOIL. THE evenings were full of talk, debates, and a songfest as a finale, with the *hora* for dessert. I spent most of the time in Gan Shmuel and rarely visited other places. I had not yet seen Jerusalem, Haifa, nor the rising town of Tel Aviv. However, the general picture of the country gradually became clearer. I realized that it was a critical period when the tiny *Yishuv* was just recovering from the effects of the first World War.

When Turkey entered the conflict on the side of Germany and Austria, all contacts with the *Yishuv* were disrupted. It was hard for Jews in the allied countries to reach the *Yishuv*. The Turks began to persecute citizens of countries at war with Turkey and there was mass expulsion. Many Jews, especially those from Russia, were expelled, including such leaders as David Ben Gurion, Yitzhak Ben Zvi, Joseph Aaronowitz, Manya Shochat and others.

The Turks confiscated Jewish property. In order to circumvent the persecutions, many Russian Jews tried to become Ottoman citizens; after strenuous efforts they succeeded, and received permission to remain in the country. The Turkish governor, General Gamal Pasha, a bitter foe of Zionism, issued an order in 1915 forbidding the use of Jewish National Fund stamps, the Zionist flag, the *Magen David* emblem. Violation could draw the death penalty. The Anglo-

Palestine Bank and other Jewish institutions were closed down. Jewish institutions that were allowed to operate were under constant surveillance. Scores of teachers, officers of organizations, leaders of the labor movement and members of *Hashomer* were exiled to Turkey. But even those who had been granted Turkish citizenship were harassed. They were not inducted into the army but sent to labor battalions to do manual work. To escape this fate one had to resort to bribery. Some were released if they could fit into another type of service needed by the Turks.

To work for the Turks was to work for starvation wages. Conditions in the labor battalions were horrible. They were the lowest echelons of the Turkish army. Weakened and swoll en by hunger, the workers wallowed in their filthy quarters, wrapped in rags and crowned with unkempt hair.

Activities of the two labor parties, *Hapoel Hatzair* and *Poale Zion*, were sharply curtailed. Their publications were outlawed.

In those days the center of action was the agricultural workers unions of Judea, Samaria and Galilee. The unions enlisted workers for the government enterprises: road building and ditch digging. Cadres of Jewish workers planted trees along the railway from Affuleh to Beersheba. In this way they got documents that exempted them from the labor battalions.

When war broke out in 1914, the export of citrus fruits and other products was halted. Unemployment was rife. Workers shared the available jobs and formed cooperative loan associations, bakeries and laundries.

Zionists in the United States formed a provisional commission for Zionist affairs with Justice Louis Brandeis as its chairman. The Commission organized an emergency fund to aid the *Yishuv* and its institutions. The first money from America arrived in Eretz Israel three months after the war erupted. It was apportioned among three districts: Jerusalem-Hebron and Motza, Jaffa and the settlements in Judea, and the Haifa-Tiberius-Safed sector, including Samaria and Galilee. Funds were allocated according to the number of workers in each region. A special committee was set up in each settlement to allot funds to each employer who would create jobs. This committee was composed of the employers and the labor organization. Luckily the aid from America continued to flow to Eretz Israel throughout the war. The United States government, through its consuls, helped greatly to make this possible.

As time went on the situation worsened. On March 26, 1917, the Turks banished 9,000 Jews from Jaffa, Tel Aviv and the Jerusalem region. Some of the displaced families settled in Petach Tikva and Kfar Saba for a while. Many went on to Galilee without any resources. The committee dealing with the uprooted people provided food while the labor offices sought jobs for them.

Half a year later the situation became catastrophic. At the command of Hassan Beck, many Jews were arrested on suspicion of disloyalty. Army patrols scoured the streets, beat up and arrested those who fell into their hands. Scores of workers and *shomrim* were tortured in the jails of Jaffa, Jerusalem, and Nazareth. About 120 were driven on foot to Damascus, many of them dying of hunger and disease. Those in the Damascus jail were mistreated horribly, some dying from their unendurable trials.

Those who remained strove to preserve the property and save Jewish possessions from the Arab plunderers. The central agricultural committees, which functioned continuously in Judea, Samaria and Galilee, made superhuman efforts to find jobs.

The history of the *Yishuv* in this period was an unbroken chain of brutal persecution by the Turks and boundless heroism among the Jews. Individuals risked their lives to alleviate the sufferings of hundred of prisoners, especially in Damascus. Two persons especially distinguished themselves in this daring activity, Avraham Harzfeld and Notte Goldberg. Joseph Bussel and others concentrated on finding jobs for the workers and refugees. Joseph Sprinzak and David Bloch played a key role in maintaining the morale of the *Yishuv*. Years later Sprinzak was to become secretary-general of the Histadrut and the first speaker of the Knesset of the State of Israel. Bloch was to become mayor of Tel Aviv. *Kupat Holim*, under the direction of Jacob Efter, served the medical needs of the people. Simultaneously, the collective settlements made phenomenal efforts to provide food for the entire *Yishuv*.

In the spring of 1916, at the initiative of Berl Katznelson, Shlomo Lavi and M. Ruthberg of Kinneret, *Hamashbir* was created to provide food for the workers at reduced prices. *Hamishbir* bought produce from the *kvutzot* and sold it with no profit. While transporting food to Judea, the wagons also bought back newspapers and books.

Avraham Harzfeld came to the country in August 1914 on the very last ship to reach Jaffa on the eve of the war. He was a young Russian revolutionary who escaped from Siberia, where he had been banished by the Russians. Harzfeld went from Jaffa to Petach Tikva, where he found work. There were vacancies, since some of the Arab workers there had been drafted into the Turkish army. As food became scarcer and the pangs of hunger increased, Harzfeld assumed the task of finding jobs and food for the needy workers. He proposed that all those with jobs should contribute five percent of their earnings to a loan fund for the unemployed. He organized a bakery and laundry, but more important, his vivacity inspired hope and confidence. The public recognized his organizational talents and elected him to the Labor Council.

Harzfeld went to Jaffa on behalf of the Labor Council, to obtain money from the Palestine Bureau for the loan fund. Later he went to Jerusalem for flour from the Turkish authorities, for the cooperative bakery. Then he made the rounds of the settlements and fostered self-help units for the unemployed.

107

In the fall of 1916 Harzfeld went up to the highlands of Galilee, intending to work in a *kvutza*. During Passover week, 1917, the Turks ordered the Jews to leave Jaffa and Tel Aviv. Refugees streamed toward Galilee, and Harzfeld organized relief for them. By the end of 1917, mass arrests occurred and Jews were transported to Damascus on suspicion that they were spies. Under torture, some·were permanently crippled and others died. When the first bits of news filtered out, Harzfeld mobilized the delivery of food and medicines to the prisoners. Armed with a false Austrian passport which he had brought along from Siberia, he set out for Damascus. Notwithstanding the fact that spoke no Turkish, Harzfeld, with the help of an interpreter and bribery, succeeded in reaching a high Turkish authority and won the right to see the prisoners, among whom were some of the top personalities of the *Yishuv*. He encouraged them and promised to do all he could to get them out.

He contacted the Jewish community in Damascus, the Palestine Bureau and the *kvutzot* in Eretz Israel for money, so he could purchase the food and medicine urgently needed. He engineered the release of some elderly prisoners and continued his activities until the British conquered Damascus in October 1918. Then he asked the British commander to allow the Jewish prisoners to return to Palestine and to furnish transportation. When the matter dragged out, Harzfeld suggested that the prisoners be permitted to go home on foot. He marched at the head of this dramatic procession.

When Histadrut, the general federation of workers in Eretz Israel, was founded in 1920, Harzfeld became head of its Agricultural Center; he devoted the rest of his life to the promotion of Jewish settlements throughout the country.

A few more facts will illumine the conditions of the *Yishuv* under Ottoman rule. At the expulsion of the Jews from Jaffa and Tel Aviv, the *Poale Zion* newspaper protested and it was shut down. The "official" editor, Zev Ashur, was arrested. Soon thereafter, David Ben Gurion and Yitzhak

Ben Zvi were detained, and after an investigation in Jerusalem, they were expelled from the country. The two comrades went to the United States where they stimulated recruitment for the Jewish Legion. They also sparked the development of the *Poale Zion* movement in America.

In Haifa, the Turks arrested Israel Schochat and Yehoshua Hankin, and they were brought to Jerusalem, accused of being members of the underground organization that wanted to tear Palestine away from the Turkish empire. After a trial they were deported to Anatolia.

Hashomer, the watchmen's society, and the general public were ordered to turn in their weapons. The *Hashomer* committee disregarded this edict and, contrarily, expanded their supply for the protection of the *Yishuv*. In addition to confiscating weapons wherever they could detect them, the Turks continued to make arrests. One of the first to be seized was Manya Shochat, who was charged with amassing arms for *Hashomer*. She was incarcerated in the Jerusalem jail for women where she was interrogated by Baha Din, an official brought especially from Constantinople. He insulted her and her "Zionism." A firebrand, Manya knew how to hold her own in debate.

Young Rachel Yanait also played an important role in *Hashomer*, *Poale Zion* and the general relief work. She visited Manya daily in prison, bribing a guard to have her transferred from a cramped twenty-foot dungeon to roomier quarters where she could receive "guests."

Manya was shipped to Damascus where she was to stand before a military tribunal. Rachel discovered that one of the judges was a Turk from the Caucasus who understood Russian. She went to the judge with a Jewish lawyer. Rachel spoke to him in Russian and the lawyer in Turkish. They convinced the judge to impose a light sentence: Manya was to join her husband to be deported to Anatolia. It was a successful intervention.

In those perilous days, Rachel Yanait travelled incessantly to help the workers in the settlements. She organized communes in Rehovot and Ness Ziona, and set up workers' kitchens and cooperative vegetable gardens everywhere.

In passing, I have mentioned a few names—Ben Gurion, Ben Zvi, Harzfeld, Rachel Yanait, Manya Shochat—personalities to whom I shall refer again. The more I learned about their fiery idealism, the more enthusiastic I became about my own participation in the movement. The conditions were truly rugged: the earth was hard, the sun was a scorcher, malaria was rampant. But in contrast there were those amazing people in the vanguard; some had been prisoners languishing in Turkish jails, others endured privation in the labor battalions. Yes, we were a free people with a free will. Among such people I too could labor like a demon.

Top row, l to r: Ceshek Rosenthal, Leib Rubinstein, Abraham Greenberg, Nathan Spivack, Jacob Dombrowski. *Middle row:* Tuvia Altman, unidentified, Yehuda Robin, Jacob Shlamowitz. *Bottom row:* Chaim Luria, Jacob Soskowski, Simcha Grossbard, —— Marcus.

The author, wearing a borrowed uniform of the Jewish Legion.

The author, with some Jewish Legionnaires from the United States, in Alexandria. The girl is the author's friend, whom he escorted to London.

Sister Frania, taken in Lodz.

The author's father, Eliezer Rubinstein.

The author's grandparents, his mother's parents.

At work in an olive grove at Hulda. The author is at left.

Members of the Hulda Kvutza. *Top row, l to r:* Jacob Zmigrod, Yehuda Rubin, Shmuel Spielman, T. Hurwitz, Leib Rubinstein, —— Pross, Yehuda Green- kop. *Middle row:* Aaron Ben Barak, Shlomo Kaiser, Chana Barash, Yitzhak Caspi, —— Machlin, Chaim Shurer, Chaim Izuz. *Bottom row:* Elizer Brown, Mrs. Feigen, Eliyahu Rachlenko, Yaffa Shaposhnik, Moshe Rothenberg, Nahum Lichterman, David Ben Yishai, Jacob Soskowski.

A scout group, with its leadership, in Zgierz. Standing at far left is the author. Fourth from left is the author's sister Frania, and beside her brother Joseph. At bottom right is the author's brother Michael.

Conference of scoutmasters of the Lodz region, September 1918. Leon Rubinstein is standing in the second row, far left.

In Trieste, the Aliyah group standing before the Central Synagogue, with the president of the Zionist Organization, Mr. Dlugatch.

Group picture taken at Ponto Luciano, near Barcotivoli, Italy. Jacob Blaustein is kneeling in the center.

Another photograph of the group, taken in Ponto Luciano.

WOMEN IN THE SECOND ALIYA

DURING THE KINNERET CONFERENCE I MET NOT ONLY THE
male delegates but also the young women and girls who represented some of the *kvutzot*. For the first time, I became
aware of the specific problems of women in the settlements.
Why were they shut in all day in the home or the kitchen
while the men and boys worked outdoors in the fresh air?
When I heard about the heroism of Manya Shochat, Rachel
Yanait and other women, I realized how narrow were the
concepts of our comrades in Lodz and Zgierz. We had given
little thought to the role of women in the building of the
homeland. The longer I lived in Gan Shmuel, the clearer became my view of women, who matched the heroism of the
men and sometimes even exceeded it.

Let us take Manya Shochat. She was born in 1880 in a
village near Grodno, of a well-to-do family. Her father, Zev
Wilbushevitz, was a mill owner and possessed some land as
well. Manya had private tutors, who taught her Hebrew and
modern languages as well as general subjects. Later she enrolled in the Grodno *gymnasium*, where she joined a group
of social revolutionaries and became an activist, organizing
factory workers to strike for better conditions and higher
wages. She also adhered to the terrorist groups of the Social Revolutionaries and undertook to raise funds for their
hidden arsenals.

111

After the Kishinev pogrom of 1903, the revolutionists plotted to assassinate the Czar's Minister of the Interior, von Plehve, who was instrumental in fomenting pogroms against the Jews. Manya went to Berlin to seek money to sent to Russia. To mask her plans, she entered a commercial academy in Berlin. She extracted a large sum from a wealthy Jew who had been born in Russia, purchased weapons, and sent them to her comrades. A provocateur exposed the conspiracy, and some of the members of the underground were killed by the secret police.

The Russian police began a search for members of the revolutionary underground, including Manya Wilbushevitz. Her brother Nahum, an industrial engineer, was then in the land of Israel, investigating the prospects for industrial enterprises in the country. When he heard that Manya was in danger, he telegraphed her that something serious had happened to him and she should come at once. She hastened to him (this was in 1904). When she found out the reason for his telegram she wanted to return at once to Russia, but her ship had already sailed from Jaffa.

Her brother then suggested that they tour the country since he had to see it for his business. Manya agreed and they rode on horseback ten hours a day, crossing the Arab terrain from Dan to Beersheba. They also visited Trans-Jordan. Thanks to this excursion, Manya became enamored of the land and decided to remain.

Manya later visited the settlements supported by Baron Rothschild and made a statistical study, to find out why they had annual deficits, why they needed assistance from the Jewish Colonization Association and what kind of improvements could be made. She met with each farmer individually and stayed in each village about two weeks. She came to the conclusion that a system of collective agricultural nuclei had to be formed. Later she went to Paris to continue her research and become familiar with collective colonization in

112

other countries. She gained entry into the French government department for colonization in Tunis and Algiers.

Meanwhile, pogroms again started to spread in Russia. A former comrade of the underground came to Paris, begging her to raise funds for Jewish self-defense. Manya raised two hundred thousand francs, including fifty thousand from Baron Rothschild. She made contact with a large munitions factory in Liege, Belgium, got weapons and smuggled them across four borders to Russia. On her last trip, disguised as a rabbi's wife from Frankfurt and using a false German passport, she brought eight large crates of weapons into Russia, although the bill of lading showed that the contents were religious books, a gift from Frankfurt Jewry to the *Yeshivas* of the Ukraine. Because of her perfect disguise and documentation, the crates were not inspected at the border. In Odessa, members of the underground were waiting for her and took over the precious shipment, which was distributed among the villages where pogroms were anticipated.

Manya participated in the defense during the Shedlitz pogrom. She spent three more months in Russia and helped form a national group sworn to take revenge against the anti-Semites. One of the comrades, Pinhas Dashevsky, shot Krushevanen, and the police arrested a number of the self-defense unit.

Manya returned to the land of Israel at the end of 1906 via Constantinople. She renewed her activities on behalf of collective colonization, especially in the Hauran, across the Jordan.

Early in 1907 she sailed to America to mobilize support for the colonization plan in Trans-Jordan as well as to get financial support for Jewish self-defense in Russia. She spent half a year in the United States, and met with Dr. Judah Magnes and Henrietta Szold. Through the mediation of Dr. Magnes, she obtained a substantial sum for self-defense but the idea of settling Jews in Trans-Jordan did not arouse any support. During her stay, she visited the settlements of the Doukhobors in western Canada and became familiar with their collective enterprises.

In August 1907 she returned to Eretz Israel and started to work at the Sedjera farm. She kept the books half a day and tended the cows the other half; she strove to implement her thoughts on agricultural collectivism. In Sedjera she suggested to the farm manager, Krause, that he hand over the agricultural work to a group that would be responsible for it under the leadership of two of their own members, who would in turn be responsible to him. Furthermore, he should employ women.

The idea was to demonstrate that Jewish workers, even under the special conditions in the country, were qualified to work collectively and reduce the constant deficits of the farm.

Krause agreed. By contract, the eighteen members took over the plowing and the dairy assignments. The farm provided the equipment, seeds, and inventory. Conditions were the same as for the Arab farmers. A fifth of the harvest was to be given to the farm, and the workers borrowed living expenses on account of the future produce.

Thanks to the driving power of the young manager of the economic enterprises, Manya Wilbushevitz, the group succeeded and Krause was satisfied. All difficulties were overcome and a collective life was established with one treasury, one account and a communal kitchen for all.

Thus was founded the first workers' collective in the country. It was named simply: *Collektiv*. Its success led to the idea of establishing a "cooperative colony."

Manya eventually married the founder of the secret *Bar Giora* defense organization (predecessor of *Hashomer*), Israel Shochat. Manya was a true example of the special breed of young women who came to the land of Israel during the Second *Aliya*. Their numbers were small and their lot was harder than that of the men. If the struggle for work was

114

difficult for the men, it was much more so for the women.

One of the very earliest women of the Second *Aliya* was Sarah Malkin. She was a member of *Bnot Zion* (Daughters of Zion) in Dvinsk and when she arrived in Israel in January 1905 she was a mere twenty years old. Like all newcomers, Sarah went to Petach Tikva, determined to work in an orange grove or with olive trees. The handful of colonists who had already agreed to hire young Jews could not understand at all why a nice Jewish daughter should want to toil like an Arab peasant woman. Even her own comrades were skeptical about a Jewish girl doing manual labor on a farm.

Sarah worked temporarily for an elderly woman, ironing the clothes that Arab women had washed. They offered her a job as a seamstress, at which she could earn more money, but she refused. In the back of her mind was the ultimate objective of becoming an agricultural worker. When harvest time came around she got her wish: to work in the orange groves, not to pick the fruit, but to sort it. She made every effort to excel and the manager of the grove was so pleased with her that he assigned her to picking the oranges. This was the acme of success. At last she had become a "conqueror" of work along with the men.

Sarah was among the founders of *Hapoel Hatzair*. After the excommunication in Petach Tikva she went to Sedjera in Galilee. In 1908, when the Palestine Bureau established the Kinneret farm, she was invited by the group that had taken over the development of the place to manage the household. She cooked and baked and stood watch in the house when the men went out to work.

When the first *kvutza*, Degania, was founded, she was among its pioneers. Sarah was one of the first students at the **agricultural school created by Hannah Meisel at Kinneret,** along with Rachel Katznelson, Rachel Bluvstein and Yael Gordon. Later, she and Yael established the girls' commune at Merhavia.

I have mentioned the name of Miriam Baratz several

115

times. She was the young woman who had given birth to a son in Degania. Let me add a few words to what I have said about her. Her maiden name was Ostrovsky. She came to the land of Israel in the month of Elul, 1906, at the age of sixteen, together with two brothers and a sister. She began working in the groves of Petach Tikva, but she did not have work every day and there were stretches of unemployment. Neverthless, she was cheerful and would sing and dance with her comrades even in bad times of unemployment and malaria.

When news came that Jewish workers were needed in Hadera to pick peas, Miriam went to Jaffa, where the colonists of Hadera were selecting suitable workers. Miriam got in line with all the men. The representatives of the landowners doubted that a woman could do the work but finally they relented and hired her. Together with twenty-two other workers she went on foot to Hadera. She was the first Jewish woman to work on the land in Hadera.

There she met Joseph Baratz and she joined the local commune. She went with the group to Um Juni, Degania. She married Baratz in 1912. Her son Gideon was the first child born in a *kvutza*. There was debate whether the mother should devote herself full time to caring for the child. Miriam was against this as she did not want to cease working in the barn. She therefore continued to work and care for the tot, getting up at three o'clock in the morning to wash the infant's clothes, work in the barn and then in the kitchen until ten o'clock.

Throughout her long life in Degania, together with Joseph, she worked and raised her children. Her routine was interrupted when she went to Holland to study dairying. Later she taught newcomers in Degania all phases of agriculture and housekeeping.

I have mentioned the fact that when Manya Shochat was imprisoned, she was visited by Rachel Yanait. Rachel, who was to marry Yitzhak Ben Zvi, a labor leader who was to become Israel's second president, was born in Russia in 1886 and joined the Zionist movement at a very early age. She was a founder of the *Poale Zion* in Russia, and a member of the self-defense. For three years, Rachel travelled from town to town, preaching the idea of self-defense against the *pogromchiks* and about the Jewish renaissance in the land of Israel. She decided to go to Eretz Israel herself and arrived in Jerusalem in 1908. She helped found a Hebrew high school where she became a history teacher.

She became an activist in *Poale Zion* and in 1910 she helped found the *Poale Zion* newspaper, *Haachdut*, becoming one of the editors, along with Ben Zvi, Ben Gurion and Jacob Zerubavel. In 1909 at a conference of *Hashomer* in Messcha, she enlisted as a member of that self-defense organization, the forerunner of *Hagana*.

Rachel went to France in 1911 to study agriculture at the university in Nancy. She returned to Eretz Israel in 1914 as an agricultural engineer.

Another young woman who left an indelible imprint on the early *Yishuv* was Hannah Meisel, who had founded the girls' agricultural school in Kinneret. She was born in Grodno and attended an agricultural school in Berlin, then proceeded to Switzerland to study natural sciences. After completing her studies she came to Israel in 1908. For a year she worked at the Sedjera farm and gave lectures on farming. In May 1911, Hannah obtained a corner of the Kinneret farm for her girls' farm school. Ten girls attended the first year. Half of the maintenance for the students came from their farm work and half from the Women's Organization for Cultural Work in Eretz Israel, which had been formed in Berlin in 1908.

The school had twenty dunam, about seven acres. The main crop was vegetables. The girls also planted saplings for fruit trees and raised cattle and poultry. In its third year, the school had twenty-two girls. One of them must be given a special citation, Rachel Bluvstein.

While my group was in Rome, we received much moral

and material support from Dr. Jacob Bluvstein, who had influential Italian friends. Through his intervention, we received certain privileges from the Italian authorities. Dr. Bluvstein's sister was Rachel, who became one of the first Hebrew poets in Eretz Israel. The life of Rachel Bluvstein reads like an absorbing novel. She was among the most colorful women in the new *Yishuv*.

Rachel was born September 20, 1890, in Saratov, in northern Russia. Her father was a soldier in Tzar Nicholas's army. In the days of Nicholas I, small Jewish boys were snatched from their homes and placed in a Christian environment so that they would convert. Rachel's father, Isser Leib Bluvstein, in spite of his youth, stubbornly clung to his Judaism that he had learned in his father's house. When he was eighteen, he was inducted into the army where he served twenty-five years. After demobilization, he began to deal in furs and prospered. He married Sonya Halberstam, the daughter of the famous Rabbi Halberstam of Riga. She was an educated woman who knew many languages and corresponded with many Russian intellectuals, including Leo Tolstoy. When Rachel was young, her parents moved to Poltava in the Ukraine, where she spent her childhood.

The Bluvstein home was dominated by a religious atmosphere, with a leaning toward *Haskala*, the enlightenment. Sonya's sons were given a higher education; those who were not accepted in Russian schools were sent abroad to study.

At first Rachel had a private tutor, then she attended a Russian *gymnasium*. She was blessed with two talents, poetry and painting. In her early years she was afflicted with a lung ailment and was sent to a sanatorium in the Crimea. Her older sister Lisa accompanied her. She wrote to their mother that Rachel would lie for hours with a book in her hands. When tired, she asked Lisa to read her Russian poems. One morning Lisa found on the table a sheet of paper on which Rachel had written her own poem, in Russian.

When their mother died, Rachel and her sister Shoshanna

went to their older sister Lisa, in Kiev, to study painting. In 1909, Rachel and Shoshanna went with other young people to Odessa where they embarked on a ship sailing to Eretz Israel. They planned to visit the land of legends and dreams and to return to Europe to continue their studies. After sailing for two weeks, they neared the ancient port of Jaffa. It was a remarkable sight that entranced the two sisters, who jumped up, raised their hands and swore that they would never forsake their motherland. They ended with a stirring *Hatikva*.

Rachel and Shoshanna went to Rehovot where they rented a room and started to study Hebrew. They visited the kindergarten of Chana Weisman to learn to speak the language directly from the children. This led to a firm friendship between the sisters and Chana. They spent their evenings together and on the Sabbath the trio went on excursions.

The sisters agreed not to speak Russian to each other, but only Hebrew. But they had a problem—they could not express everything in their new tongue. They compromised by speaking Russian one hour a day, and they would recite Russian poetry.

Soon their younger sister, Bathsheba, who had been studying piano in Leipzig, came to Eretz Israel. Their father sent them funds all the while, so they could afford a piano. In the evenings, after working in the gardens and fields, the workers would meet in the home of the three sisters and sing, with Bathsheba at the piano.

When Rachel felt that she had acquired the rudiments of Hebrew, she decided to study farming, Seeking a place to learn, she was told to see Chana Meisel at Sedjera. On the way she spent the night at a Haifa hotel, where she learned that Meisel was in Haifa and she called on her.

Chana spoke to her boss, Eliahu Blumenfeld, an agronomist who had brought her from Sedjera to work in his olive grove near Mount Carmel. Blumenfeld refused to hire Rachel as he did not believe that such a refined girl could do farm work, but he allowed her to share a room with Chana. Rachel worked without pay in the olive groves and among the almond trees and pines. Near the house she tended the vegetable garden and planted flowers. The earth in which the olive trees were planted was caked and stone-covered; the older trees had been neglected and were hard to take care of. Rachel and Chana came home exhausted and still had to tend their own patch and get meals ready for the next day. Rachel never complained. She did not feel lonely; on the contrary, she was gay and would recite aloud from the Bible and quote Hebrew poetry.

She loved nature, the land and the workers on the land. She strove to get inured to manual labor with her delicate hands, to master the hoe and the shears. She expressed her love of nature in a poem, *Ganeinu*, our garden.

That winter, Sedjera was without a planting specialist. Eliahu Krause, the agronomist, asked Blumenfeld to allow Chana to come to Sedjera and she agreed, on the condition that Rachel also come along and be assigned to pruning grapevines. In 1911, Chana and Rachel left Haifa for Kinneret, where Chana organized the first permanent agricultural school for girls. Rachel was the first student. Enamored of the Kinneret, she imbibed the magical panorama.

Rachel wrote in her notebook: Al Sfat Hakinneret, on the shores of the Kinneret:

How does the day pass in Kinneret? At sunrise we fourteen girls started our work, our hands calloused, our barefoot legs tanned and full of scratches, our faces cheerful, our hearts flaming. The air was filled with the sounds of our songs and laughter. We worked unceasingly, pausing only to wipe the sweat from our foreheads, with our shirtsleeves. We enjoyed the sight of the indescribable blue of Lake Kinneret. Sometimes we would see a sailboat or the small steamer that carried passengers from Tzemach to Tiberias. At noon, when we returned to the farm, the lake was still with us, its azure blue just beyond the window of our dining room.

Even though our meals were meager, our voices were loud and full of joy. Not only is Lake Kinneret a beautiful piece of nature but the destiny of our people is connected with its name. It has witnessed our past. On Shabbat, we used to go out to rest on the nearby hills which had winding crevices that gave us many hiding places. One is tempted to remain here all of one's life. How pleasant it is to stroll along the shores of Lake Kinneret till the walls of Tiberias with their round towers become visible. Tiberias is so old that it does not look like a city in which people live but like an illustration in a textbook of ancient history.

Look, these stones have seen the pale face of the preacher of Nazareth. They have heard the studious discussions of the Tannaim. The ash-colored stones remember the beautiful face of Berenica, the sweetheart of Herod.

Rachel did well and Chana Meisel induced her to go to France to get a degree in agriculture. In 1913 Rachel went to Toulouse in southern France, where she completed her studies with distinction.

With the outbreak of the war, Rachel could not return to Eretz Israel, and she could not remain in France, so she returned to Russia. At first she lived with her family, doing miscellaneous work to earn her keep. Finally she undertook to care for refugee children in Odessa.

In 1919 she returned to Eretz Israel on the first boat from Odessa, the *Russlan*. Her lung sickness recurred, but she minimized it and began working in Degania. The *kvutza* assigned her to lighter tasks, to watch over the children. Her illness became more acute, but she did not go to a doctor. When she became extremely ill, a doctor was summoned from Tiberias, who diagnosed the case: she had advanced tuberculosis. He forbade her working with children.

Rachel was forced to leave her Degania and her Kinneret. She went to Petach Tikva to teach agriculture. Later she went

121

to Jerusalem to teach Hebrew, French and farming. When her illness deepened and she had to give up teaching in the school, she gave private lessons. She then spent several months at the hospital in Safed, high in the fresh Galileean air. Leaving the hospital she went to Tel Aviv, to live for a time with her brother, Dr. Jacob Bluvstein.

As her illness progressed, Dr. Moshe Beilinson placed her in a sanatorium in Gedera. Feeling that she had little time left, she demanded a transfer to Tel Aviv, where she would not be isolated from her friends. On April 15, 1941, she died in the Hadassah hospital and was buried in accordance with her wishes, at Kinneret.

She left many beautiful poems, of which four are reprinted here: (translation by Morris Samuel)

IN THE GARDEN

Calm is the garden with blue and gray
   In the peace of dawn.
I will rise from the dust of yesterday
   To faith in the morn,
Accept with humble heart and free
The Judgment that was given me.

A girl walks through the garden beds
   And scatters rain;
The withered leaves lift up their heads
   And live again.
The bitter things that God must do
I will forgive and start anew.

MY MOTHERLAND

No deeds of high courage,
No poems of flame,

I bring you, my country,
To add to your fame;
By Jordan I planted
A tree in your soil,
And I wore out a path
In the field of my toil

Well knows your daughter,
My own motherland,
How poor is her tribute,
How weak is her hand.
But my heart shouts with joy
When the sun shines upon you,
And in secret I weep
For the wrong that is done you.

VEULAI
(PERHAPS)

Perhaps these things have never been at all!
   Perhaps that life was not!
Perhaps I never answered morning's earliest call
   To sweat in labor on my garden plot!

Perhaps I never stood upon the loaded cart
   To gather up the hay
Nor heard the wild songs bursting from my heart
   The livelong harvest day!

Perhaps I never made my body whole
   In the blue and quiet gleam
Of my Kinneret! Oh, Kinneret of my soul,
   Were you once true, or have I dreamed a dream?

BARREN

Oh, if I had a son, a little son,
With black curled hair and clever eyes,
A little son to walk with in the garden
Under morning skies,
A son,
A little son!

I'd call him Uri, little, laughing Uri,
A tender name as light, as full of joy
As sunlight on the dew, as tripping on the tongue
As the laughter of a boy—
"Uri!"
I'd call him.

And still I wait, as mother Rachel waited,
Or Hannah in Shiloh, she, the barren one,
Until the day comes when my lips will whisper,
"Uri, my son!"

Rachel the poet will forever remain as a bright and moving star in the history of modern Israel. Another young woman, also named Rachel, was likewise a builder of the land. She was Rachel Katznelson, who was to become the wife of Zalman Rubashov (Shazar), in later years to become the third president of the State of Israel.

Rachel Katznelson was born in 1888 in Bobroisk, Russia. She was graduated from a Russian *gymnasium*, and then studied in Berlin at the Academy for Jewish Studies. She learned German and German literature.

On returning to Russia, Rachel continued her education at Baron Guinzburg's Institute for Jewish Studies in Petrograd. She became a teacher for a while, but she was attracted to Zionism, and in 1912 went to Eretz Israel. She taught Hebrew at the Kinneret girls' school and at the same time studied agriculture under Chana Meisel.

Until 1917, Rachel worked in the *kvutzot* of Galilee and also in Jerusalem. When *Ahdut Avoda* was founded the next year, she became a member of the party's cultural committee. She married Zalman Rubashov in 1920.

When the general labor federation, Histadrut, was founded in December 1920, Rachel became a member of its cultural committee and later editor of the women's journal, *Dvar Hapoelet*, a supplement to the labor daily, *Davar*.

Another young woman who was to become celebrated in Hebrew literature came to Eretz Israel in 1911, Dvora Baron. She was born in the *shtetl* of Azda in the Minsk province, where her father Shabtai Baron was the rabbi. Dvora was active in a Hebrew-speaking club at the high school. While still in school, she published short stories in *Hamelitz* and *Hatzfira*, the outstanding Hebrew periodicals of the day. Her writings drew the attention of editors and literary critics, who praised her highly.

Upon arrival in Eretz Israel she became a Hebrew teacher and for a time was a staff member of *Hapoel Hatzair*, serving as the paper's literary editor. She succeeded in attracting the best literary talents in the country and encouraged young writers to contribute to the paper.

Dvora married the paper's editor, Yosef Aaronowitz. She herself enriched Hebrew literature by depicting the idyllic side of the Lithuanian *shtetl*, the materially difficult but spiritually rich life.

I have already mentioned the secretary of the Kinneret conference, Ada Fishman. She was an observant, orthodox Jewess, who put aside her pen when Sabbath arrived. Ada, the sister of Rabbi Yehuda Leib Fishman, was born in Bessarabia in 1893. In 1912, at the age of nineteen, she arrived in Eretz Israel, and began her working career in Petach Tikva in the field. In 1914 she went to Safed to establish a girls' school. The first to devote herself full time to the women's labor movement, she was active in the *Hapoel Hatzair* party and was elected to its central committee in 1914. When Histadrut was founded, she became secretary of *Moetzet Hapoalot*, the working women's council. In 1930 she became director of the girls' farm school, Ayanot. She wrote many articles and several books.

These were only a few of the girls who came to the country, driven by the dream of *Shivat Zion*, the return to Zion. They all endured the hardship of climate and hard work as did the men, but they had the added burden of proving that they were not the "weaker sex." In some instances they outpaced their men comrades. At any rate, they were equals in their heroism.

Most of them came at the dawn of the Second *Aliya*. In 1914, on the eve of World War I, they convoked the first conference of working women, with some thirty delegates representing 210 members in Galilee and Judea. That may seem to be an insignificant number, but taking into account the conditions in the land, it was rather substantial.

When I arrived in Eretz Israel with my Lodz group as the harbingers of the Third *Aliya*, all the women I have mentioned here were still alive. I had the privilege of meeting some of them in person, and they won my great admiration.

PIONEERS OF THE SECOND ALIYA

THE HEAT THAT SUMMER WAS FIERCE. THE SUN POURED ITS rays upon us, and we sought relief after work by plunging into a pool that was used for irrigating the trees. It was a dirty pool, and I talked to the leading comrades about cleaning it up, but it was not an easy matter. It was the height of the season and no manpower could be spared. They told me that if I wished, I could do the job myself. I did it with diligence, working with a bucket to extract the messy material and in several days, with a calloused pair of hands, I had clear water in which it was a pleasure to bathe after a day's work. It was only then that I picked up my hoe and returned to tending the trees.

During my stay in Gan Shmuel, I developed a broad view of the entire country and became acquainted with the extraordinary individuals who shaped it.

Eliezer Shochat came to the country early in 1904 at the age of thirty, together with his younger brother, Israel. As was customary, they went to work in Petach Tikva. Eliezer, a quiet man, was impressively handsome, a deep thinker, simple in manner, honest and with an iron will. He was a key organizer of the workers in Judea, and was among the initiators of meetings where the workers were exhorted to struggle for *kibbush ha'avoda*, the conquest of labor, and for mutual aid. He was a founder of *Hapoel Hatzair* and helped formulate its program.

Not satisfied with working only in the vineyards and orange groves, Eliezer took the first opportunity, in 1906, to go to Sedjera together with other *Hapoel Hatzair* comrades to farm. He founded the first non-partisan organization of agricultural workers in Galilee, *HaHoresh* (The Plowman) during *Sukkot* 1907. That same year, *Hapoel Hatzair* launched its own newspaper, in which the labor personalities expressed their views. Eliezer wrote on many issues of the day, his first article being published in 1911. He was aided immeasurably by his close friend, Shlomo Zemach, especially in promoting the development of agricultural workers, a stratum of Jewish labor that did not exist in the Diaspora.

Zemach was born in Plonsk, Poland, on June 2, 1886, of a scholarly family that descended from Rabbi Hirsch Halevi Plinsk, author of *Zemach L'Avraham* (The Plant of Abraham), from which the family adopted its name. Shlomo's father, Avraham, was well-established in the village of Wolkow. There Shlomo spent his childhood, from age three to eight; he was reared in an agricultural environment which never left his bloodstream.

His father was a *Gerer Hassid*, and Shlomo prayed with him in the *Gerer Shtibl*. He wore silk garb and lived like all the other *Hassidic* children. At his *bar mitzva*, his father sent him to the Gerer rabbi, known as the *Sfat Emes*, during the *Shavuot* festival. Shlomo was an only son, and studied the Talmud, first with a private tutor and then at the *Beth ha midrash* where he prepared for the rabbinate. Shlomo and his sister also studied Hebrew and German at home with a tutor who was a member of *Hovevei Zion*, the Lovers of Zion, who influenced him toward Zionist thought and toward a love of the Hebrew tongue.

In 1900, together with another native of Plonsk, David Green (later David Ben Gurion), Shlomo Lefkowitz (Lavi) and Lipa Taub, who were all of the same age (about fifteen years old) and several other friends, he founded the *Ezra* club.

Shlomo Zemach decided at the age of eighteen that he had to join the builders of the Jewish homeland. Without his father's knowledge he took from him 300 rubles and without saying goodbye left home and the benches of the *beth ha midrash* for a boat that would bear him to Eretz Israel. He was the first *Ezra* member to leave Plonsk for *Aliya*, the first *Halutz* from Russian-Poland to join the Second *Aliya*. Almost all the others were to follow him eventually.

It was hard to find a job because of the hostile attitude of the Jewish landowners toward Jewish workers. He was especially upset when he learned that many of the colonists were "ugandists," adhering to Theodor Herzl's project to create a temporary Jewish colony in Africa, an "asylum for the night." The colonists, at a public meeting, railed against Zionism and supported the Uganda venture.

Shlomo Zemach could not restrain himself and strongly protested the calumny and the betrayal of Zionism. He shouted: "Don't look down on me because I am so young! I will fight you and all who malign Zionism, not with words but with my two hands which I have brought to oppose your scores of hands which do nothing. I shall fight with hands of deeds, of construction."

Zemach found employment in a vineyard where he was also a watchman. Eventually he met Aaron David Gordon and Eliezer Shochat, and during a meeting the idea arose to convene the isolated workers in the various settlements to consider an organization that would improve their lot. In October 1905 the *Hapoel Hatzair* party was born. Helping to shape its program, Zemach coined the phrase *kibbush ha'-avoda*, which became the motto of the Second *Aliya*.

After Shochat had moved to Galilee in 1906, Zemach followed him and they formed *HaHoresh*. In 1907, Zemach went to study in France at the Nancy agricultural institute where he graduated as an agricultural engineer. When World War I broke out, he could not return to Eretz Israel, so he went to Poland, where he taught Hebrew for a time at the

Warsaw *gymnasium*, *Hinuch*, and was active in the Zionist movement. When he returned to Eretz Israel, he became a teacher at the *Mikveh Yisrael* agricultural school.

Zemach returned with a full array of new methods of farmwork. He suggested experiments in growing more vegetables and grain on smaller plots of fertile soil through irrigation. He was convinced that with new methods more than one crop could be raised during the year. The older agronomists were skeptical, but Zemach went ahead on his own responsibility and he succeeded.

He became director of the Agricultural Department of the Zionist Organization, serving nine years. In 1933, he founded the Kadoorie Agricultural School on Mount Tabor, which he directed for four years. He was also one of the first Hebrew writers in the country, and was prolific as well as excellent in his literary endeavors, which included stories and essays. He was a literary critic and also published books on agricultural topics. For a time he edited the literary magazine, *Moznaim*.

An outstanding personality of this period was Yehoshua Hankin, a pioneer among pioneers. He came to Eretz Israel when the first contingents of *Biluim* came, in 1882, at the age of seventeen, with his parents, four brothers and five sisters. His father, Leib, was a founder of Rishon L'Zion. The other settlers, unable to withstand the grueling hardships, accepted aid from Baron Rothschild. The Baron's agents were paternalistic overseers, and laid down strict rules. Leib Hankin did not need the Baron's help and disliked the conduct of the Baron's agents. He sold his land and moved to Gedera.

Yehoshua cemented friendly relations with the Arab landowners and peasants. He learned their language and customs and manner of speech. With his charismatic personality, he won the confidence of the Arabs and was able to buy land from them for Jewish settlements.

In 1890, Hankin bought ten thousand dunams of land and sold them to the *Menucha V'Nachala* society which founded the town of Rehovot. In 1891, he bought thirty thousand dunams in Samaria and sold them to settlement agents from Riga, Kovno and other Russian towns. Hadera was established on this land. The scope of Hankin's land purchases was enormous by the standards of those days. In time he became the acknowledged expert in this field. He could wend his way through the tangle of Turkish land regulations to make purchases and register ownership in the name of Jewish proprietors.

He entered Baron Rothschild's service to purchase land. Later he did the same for the Jewish Colonization Association (ICA). Thanks to his efforts, land was acquired in Upper Galilee and other sections of the country. When the Palestine Land Development Company, *Hachsharat Hayishuv*, was created in 1908, Dr. Arthur Ruppin invited Hankin to represent the company in land deals for it and for the Jewish National Fund in the Valley of Esdraelon, the Emek.

Despite great complications and strong hostile propaganda emanating from the Christians of Nazareth against the sale of land to Jews and the settling of Jews in the village of Fulah, he overcame the resistance. In 1909, thanks to his cordial relations with Turkish officials, he bought ten thousand dunams on which the first settlement point in the Emek was to be fixed, Merhavia, and subsequently, another point, Tel Adash.

Under Turkish law, a farmer who had worked his land for three years could not be dispossessed. The owners would circumvent the law by transferring their peasants to other stretches every two years. This was the case at Fulah that the *Hachsharat Hayishuv* had bought from Sheikh Murkuse. The watchmen of the area were Arabs. They were replaced by Jewish watchmen, who were to protect the building materials for the homes and farm structures, the machinery and food supplies. The Ottoman ruler of Nazareth, who opposed the Jewish settlement venture, sent police to expel the Jewish guards from the site.

The guards were driven out in the morning but they returned at night. This kept on for several weeks. The *Kaymakam*, the local headman of Nazareth, did not obey the orders of the central Turkish authorities. He argued that the holy *Hedjaz* train went through that way and alien people could not settle there. Yehoshua Hankin hit upon an idea: he simply "converted" the young Jews from the Ukraine, Lithuania and Poland into Ottoman citizens who were supposedly born in Jaffa, Safed, Haifa and Tiberias. It took a long time and a lot of money to complete this "conversion." At last, in 1911, the members of the *kvutza* came with their horses, wagons and plows to Fulah. With the help of comrades from Degania, Sedjera and Messcha they began to sow grain.

Each morning they set out with twenty-four teams of horses harnessed to wagons loaded with plows, and labored long hours. Every day they sowed from 200 to 250 dunam of land. Soon great black patches were visible, sown with winter grains. Each field was transformed into a black sea which in a few weeks would turn green.

It was peaceful and quiet for a while, but soon leaders from the neighboring Arab villages appeared, offering their protection, if not for the settlers, then for their fields. When it was explained that the *kvutza* was based on self-labor and self-defense, the Arabs gave a "friendly" warning, that this could not be in this region, for without their protection the neighbors would pounce upon the Jewish watchmen and take away their guns and horses.

When the wheat was high and in full bloom, when the oats were ripe and the *kvutza* got ready for the harvest, the first attack on the settlement took place. It happened in the evening just as supper was ending. Yigal, the Shomer, set out as usual to patrol the fields on horseback, and the *kvutza* committee sat down to plan the next day's work schedule. Suddenly there were two shots. They knew that the shots had come from Yigal's Mauser, and in a few minutes Yigal came riding on his wounded steed, calling out that among the Arabs there was a dead man.

Lights were quickly extinguished in the entire *kvutza*. All entrances to the mound were barricaded with plows and other equipment. A rider was dispatched to Nazareth to inform the government of what had transpired. About twenty minutes later, the Arabs retrieved the body of the dead man and began to mobilize the Arabs of the surrounding communities. Shouts for revenge arose from the crowd. When they neared the hillside, one of the guards fired in the air, over the heads of the approaching Arabs. A hush fell; it was still all night, but the place was beleagured.

Before daylight a horde of Arabs encircled the settlement, but they dared not come too close. Meanwhile the Nazareth police arrived and the comrades hid their weapons. The Arabs succeeded in penetrating the farm, raiding a few huts, loading some fresh-cut barley on their donkeys and on the heads of their womenfolk and trampling on the grain in the fields. The police witnessed all this but looked aside. The investigating *judge arrested fourteen members of the* kvutza and took them to Nazareth for interrogation. After two days, seven were set free and the others were detained for more interrogation. This meant that a deal had to be struck with the judge, a bribe of four hundred francs.

The comrades, together with Hankin, refused to pay ransom, and the seven arrested members were sent to the Acre prison, accused of murder, and they were cruelly tortured. After eleven months, compensation was paid to the family of the dead man and the prisoners were released. The Arabs were thus satisfied and they agreed that Fula should become a Jewish settlement. Its name became Merchavia.

HASHOMER AND THE JEWISH HERDSMEN

WHEN THE SECOND *ALIYA* ARRIVED IN THE COUNTRY, JEW-
ish settlements were scattered all over the land and it frequently happened that neighboring Arabs or wandering
Bedouins would sneak in by night to purloin whatever was
not nailed down. The loot might be chickens, horses or cows,
sometimes produce or grain. Usually, the settlers would not
guard their own domain but would hire Arab watchmen to
ward off the uninvited guests. That was how it was in the
early days, but, when I arrived in 1919, the situation had altered. Most of the settlements were protected by *Hashomer*.

Jewish self-defense was born during Sukkot, the feast
of Tabernacles, in 1907, when eight members of *Poale Zion*
gathered in the home of Yitzhak Ben Zvi in an orchard near
Jaffa. They formed a watchmen's association, *Bar Giora*,
named after the commander of the revolt against the Romans
in the days of the Second Temple.

Besides Ben Zvi there were Yechezkel Hankin, Israel Giladi, Mendel Portugali, Berl Schweiger, Yehezkel Nisanov, Zvi
Becker, Alexander Zeid and Israel Shochat. At intervals new
members joined. Some of the *Bar Giora* belonged to the *Collektiv* in Sedjera. They applied to the manager to hand over
the guarding of the farm to *Bar Giora*, to replace the Circas-
sians. Krause protested at first but soon gave in to the *Bar
Giora* request; later *Bar Giora* also assumed responsibility for
the defense of the entire settlement.

After Sedjera, the nearby settlement of Messcha also came under the wing of *Bar Giora*. During Passover, 1909, a conference was held at Messcha, with twenty-six *Bar Giora* members participating. New members were added and the organization's name was changed to *Hashomer*. Soon afterwards, the first members of *Hashomer* fell in the line of duty, Berl (Dov) Schweiger and Israel Korngold.

When the self-defense pattern was firmly established in Galilee and the entire *Yishuv* began to talk about the heroism of *Hashomer*, its membership soared. The center of *Hashomer* was in Galilee but its emissaries deployed among the workers in Samaria and Judea, enlisting many to accompany them back to Galilee.

Hashomer was based on absolute discipline. Once a year a general assembly was convened, the highest forum of the organization. Decisions were adopted by majority vote. A committee was elected, including a chairman whose orders were to be obeyed by all the *Shomrim*. Each new member had to be confirmed at the annual conference, after he had undergone a test period. He had to demonstrate his capabilities as a watchman and pass moral muster. The candidate would be put through paces that would prove his mettle in dangerous situations. One candidate related afterwards:

It was a dark night and the rains did not stop all night. I was on guard since five in the afternoon. I heard in the distance the whistle of the chief of the guard unit and ran to my assigned spot; there before me stood comrade Zvi who ordered me to go at once to Yisrulik (Israel Giladi), the commander of *Hashomer*, who lived in a small room where he had been lying sick for several days. "Listen, Chaim," Yisrulik said to me in a quiet voice, "you must have heard about the dangerous roads these days. I have an important message for Kinneret for you to deliver. It is now nine o'clock and you have to get back to me in four hours with a reply. If you encounter anything along the

135

way, remember what we have taught you: be fearless. Remember, you belong to *Hashomer*."

I left the settlement. A strong wind almost bowled me over. I loaded my rifle and went into the darkness. Fear seized me as I ventured into the wilderness, the darkness of the night. Suddenly I heard behind me a galloping horse, which came nearer and nearer. I readied my rifle and turned around. My heart throbbed and as the galloping horse came nearer, I was prepared. "Chaim!" I heard a call. I recognized the voice of my comrade watchman. He had come to tell me that the letter was no longer needed and that I should return to my post. . . . The whole thing was only a way of testing me; the letter was an excuse.

Slowly, *Hashomer* penetrated many settlements in Judea and Samaria, Rehovot, Rishon L'Zion, Hadera and others, where daily robberies took place. In addition to pilfering grain, cows, horses, machinery and tools, the Arabs would vandalize the orchards, tearing out almond saplings and vines. Because of the marauders, it was unsafe to walk the streets of the settlements at night.

When the first *shomrim* rode into town on their horses, things changed. Armed with shining rifles, they began to take over the guard duties. The Arab watchmen fought the *shomrim*, attacking in the dark, trying to steal their weapons, but they were repulsed. The *shomrim* showed steadfast resistance and became permanent fixtures in the settlements. They saw to it that the Bedouin tents should be as far as possible from the Jewish settlements and the Arab workers in the settlements were subject to a night curfew. The barns in which the Arabs slept were locked so that they could not remove their stolen goods and pass them on to accomplices waiting outside.

With the advent of the *shomrim* a new atmosphere prevailed in the settlements. Now people could stroll in the streets at night without fear. Soon there were almost no attacks or robberies.

Another problem that concerned the Jewish settlements in those days was the pasturing of their livestock. In the spring months, after the rains, when the grass had grown tall in the fields, the Jewish settlers would sent their animals—oxen, cows, mules, horses, donkeys and goats—to pasture under the aegis of Arab herdsmen. *Hashomer* felt that they had to assume this role, too, but it was not a simple matter. Ben Gurion tells in his memoirs:

After we had won the right to be watchmen in the farm and the settlement of Sedjera, the road was open for us to take over the key stronghold of the defense, the pastures. To pasture at night was not as easy as to pasture by day. One or two herdsmen were not sufficient to herd the flocks. Armed watchmen were needed. Here among the hills one could not let the flocks roam unattended in the darkness. Whole groups of watchmen, afoot and on horseback, armed from head to toe, were spread out in the valley, ears alert for every movement, eyes cutting through the darkness and watching every shadow. The hand was on the gun, ready to meet at any moment an uninvited guest.

The *shomrim* formed a special group called *Haroeh*, the shepherd. Its aim was to learn the art of pasturing the flocks and to develop sheep rearing in the Jewish economy. Understandably, many problems had to be surmounted. First, unfamiliarity with the new vocation: one did not know the different grasses and their worth. One did not know how to react to cattle diseases. Secondly, the question of claims. It was clear that the Arab shepherds would not relinquish their positions, which they declared to be their own domain. We figured that they would attack us every inch of the way.

Thirdly: the paltry wages and the prejudice of the Jewish colonists that Jews could not succeed in this type of work and that this could cause a danger to the settlement and their property.

But the idea of assuming the role of herdsmen also triumphed. In the winter of 1913, *Hashomer* sent three comrades to the Turkoman tribe which lived in the hills and pastured their sheep there, to learn the trade. The three dressed as Bedouins and went to live as Bedouin shepherds. After a year among the Turkomen, more comrades joined the group and formed *Haroeh*. The first results came swiftly. A Jewish colonist in Mitzpeh agreed to hand his flock over to *Haroeh*. Likewise in Beth Gan. Gradually other colonies followed suit.

The rise of *Hashomer* during the Second *Aliya* was of historic significance. Because of *Hashomer* the Arabs completely changed their attitude toward the Jews, who had convinced their Arab natives that they would not buy their security through intermediaries or the payment of ransom but that they could defend themselves proudly and without fear.

The idea of Jewish self-defense also had its educational merit for the children of the Jewish settlers. *Hashomer* became a legendary force among Jewish youth in the Diaspora, who read of the exploits and heroism of *Shomrim* who sacrificed their lives in defense of Jewish positions and the honor of the *Yishuv*.

When Jewish scout organizations sprang up during the first World War in Austria they called themselves, proudly, *Hashomer Hatzair*, the Young Guard. The name was adopted later by various Jewish scout groups in Poland as a symbol of respect for the Israeli *Hashomer*, whose example inspired youth inside the country and throughout the world.

"NILI"

DURING THE FIRST WORLD WAR JEWS SUFFERED THE BRU-
tality of the Ottoman regime. Some were arrested on suspicion of disloyalty, mostly on false charges. But in a few cases
there was ground for the suspicion. A Jewish espionage ring
did exist, to abet the British army that had come to the Middle East to fight the Turks.

At war's start, when persecution and mass deportations of
Jews began, a group of young Jews launched their spying activities. They called themselves *Nili*, an acronym for *Netzah
Israel Lo Yishaker*, the glory of Israel will not fail. Its leader
was Avshalom Feinberg, a son of the well-known Lulik Feinberg, who had been among the founders of Rishon L'Zion,
and later a founder of Hadera. Avshalom was friendly with
the Bedouins of the region and mastered their language and
their customs. He told his plans to form a spy ring to his
friend Alex Aaronsohn of Zichron Yaacov. They both went
to Egypt, where they were received by the British general
staff. At first the British were cool to the idea, but finally
agreed to establish contact with *Nili*. Under the cloak of
darkness a British vessel returned the two to the Palestine
shore.

Alex went to the agricultural experimental station at Athlit which was directed by his older brother, Aaron, and told
him of the developments. Aaron, who had come to the country as a six-year-old with his parents, devoted himself to

139

farming from early youth. He studied in France and California, becoming a specialist in scientific agriculture. On returning to Eretz Israel, he started the research station at Athlit with the financial backing of the Chicago philanthropist, Julius Rosenwald.

Aaron agreed to the espionage plan and became *Nili*'s leader. He drew into the network his sister Sarah, and a former *Shomer*, Joseph Lishansky. Other members included Naaman Belkind from Rishon L'Zion, Runia Mazia, son of a well-known doctor in Judea, and Ruben Schwartz, son of a Zichron Yaacov colonist. Ruben was an assistant at the experimental station.

Aaronsohn had a golden opportunity to spy, as he had excellent contacts with the Turkish military. When Palestine was attacked by locusts, Gamal Pasha appointed Aaronsohn to lead the counterattack. Aaronsohn impressed Gamal Pasha with his prowess and he met high ranking Turkish officers. In addition, Aaronsohn's experimental station served as a perfect contact point for British ships that came near the coast. Later he went to Egypt, where he lived near the general staff. Sarah and Joseph Lishansky carried on the espionage activities within Palestine.

Although the spy ring's security was tight, it was impossible to black out the news of its existence and its activities. Most of the *Yishuv* leaders were against *Nili*, being afraid that it would endanger the entire Jewish community. But as the Turkish repression grew more severe, the opposition of the established Jewish leadership weakened.

Avshalom Feinberg and Lishansky tried to smuggle through El Arish on the way to Egypt, in January 1917. Though dressed as Bedouins, they were spotted by some Bedouins and in a gun battle Feinberg was killed. Despite his wounds, Lishansky was able to cross the border and was found by a mounted Australian patrol. After a long recuperative period, Lishansky came home to resume his spying activities.

Nili came to an evil end. In September 1917, a Turkish patrol captured a carrier pigeon that was bringing a message to the British in Egypt. The Turks launched an intensive investigation, and in two weeks caught Naaman Belkind when he tried to cross the border at Beersheba. Belkind was shipped to the Damascus prison where he was tortured terribly, until he divulged information about *Nili*.

On the first day of Sukkot, Zichron Yaacov was surrounded by Turkish police and soldiers. No one was allowed to enter or leave the village. The military commander from Nazateth summoned the elders of the community and demanded that they deliver Sarah Aaronsohn and her family, Joseph Lishansky, Ruben Schwartz and other young people of Zichron Yaacov and Hadera.

Lishansky and some others escaped. Sarah and her elderly father stayed at home to face the consequences. She and her maid were arrested. The Turkish commander insisted that they deliver the others on their list. Since this was impossible, the Jewish elders were dragged into the street and beaten mercilessly. The screams were heartbreaking. Some wives caught a *Nili* member and turned him over to the Turks, who then ended the torture of the old men.

Sarah was tortured most cruelly for three days. They tried to force the *Nili* secrets out of her, and find out where Lishansky was hiding, but she endured all the torment without revealing a thing. Sarah was to be transferred to Nazareth for further interrogation. She asked to be allowed to change her bloodstained clothing and went into a room while her captors remained outside the door. Taking a revolver from a drawer, she shot herself in the throat. Attempts by doctors to save her life failed.

Lishansky was later captured and tortured in Damascus. To put an end to his agony, he gave out names of *Nili* members and of people entirely innocent. He named leaders of *Hashomer* who were not associated at all with *Nili*. Apparently, he was trying to settle old scores. They were all arrested,

141

and at a face-to-face confrontation with Lishansky, categorically denied his accusations. Believed by the Turks, they were freed. Lishansky and Belkind were hanged in public. Other *Nili* leaders were also arrested and sentenced to death.

The Turkish army increased the terror against the *Yishuv*. Hundreds were arrested, jailed, tortured. The prisoners were liberated when the British conquered Judea and Galilee.

Accompanying the British troops were two units of the Jewish Legion—the 38th and 39th Battalions, Royal Fusiliers, composed of volunteers from England and America. Some exiles living in Egypt also signed up for the Legion.

Among those arriving from America were David Ben Gurion and Yitzhak Ben Zvi, who had been among the organizers of the Legion in the United States and Canada. In Palestine, in mid-1918, the 40th Battalion, Royal Fusiliers, was formed in liberated Judea. Among the volunteers were Berl Katznelson, Eliezer Shochat, Levi Eshkol (Shkolnik) and students of the Jaffa *gymnasium*.

When I came to Eretz Israel at the beginning of 1919, the *Yishuv* had begun to breathe more freely after the suffocating years of the Ottoman regime. But the *Yishuv* was still exhausted, impoverished and suffering from a lack of commodities. Most important, the British military occupation administration was hostile to Zionism and the idea of building the Jewish homeland, in spite of the solemn undertaking of their Balfour Declaration.

HEBREW RENAISSANCE

I HAVE MENTIONED THAT ON THE RIDE FROM CAIRO TO Eretz Israel, one of our fellow passengers on the train was Eliezer Ben Yehuda. Immediately upon arrival in the country, I realized what a superhuman task it must have been for this pioneer of spoken Hebrew, together with his first colleagues, to transform the Biblical tongue into a living language, and how essential it was to erase the linguistic chaos that then prevailed in Eretz Israel.

When the first *Biluim* came in 1882 to Jaffa port, there was literally a babel of tongues. The Jews used at least a dozen languages. Most of the old *Yishuv*, about 25,000 strong, lived in the four principal cities: Jerusalem, Safed, Tiberias and Hebron; others lived in Arab-dominated cities such as Haifa and Jaffa.

Many Ashkenazic Jews spoke Yiddish; the Sephardim spoke Hebrew and Ladino, a Spanish dialect written with Hebrew script. The Yemenites spoke Hebrew. Those from Ethiopia, Bukhara, Afghanistan, India, Iraq, Libya, Tunisia and Egypt came with their respective languages and dialects. The Askenazim were pious, observant Jews, adhering to the customs of their old home. They maintained *chedorim* and *yeshivot* for their children, and translated the Bible and Talmud into Yiddish. The Sephardim had their own schools, the so-called *Kotuv*, where they read the Bible and Talmud in their own accent, or in Ladino. All these schools were only for boys; girls were excluded.

Another network of schools began to take root at the initiative of philanthropic organizations. At the time of the Turkish empire, European powers waged a *kulturkampf*: the French and the Germans were especially involved in this cultural struggle. In 1856, an Austrian woman, the daughter of Simon von Lemmel, started a school in Jerusalem with German as the language of instruction. It was named after her father: Lemmel. Almost simultaneously, Evelina de Rothschild established a school in Jerusalem with French as the basic language; this school broke with tradition: it was for girls. Other French-speaking schools were eventually opened by the Alliance Israelite Universelle.

The Alliance was established in France in 1860 for the purpose of helping needy Jews and to fight discrimination around the world. Among its founders was the prominent Jewish statesman Adolph Cremieux, who had championed Jewish rights all his life. As the French Minister of Justice, Cremieux proclaimed the complete emancipation of the Jews of Algeria in 1870. That same year the Alliance, under the presidency of Cremieux, and the prompting of Charles Netter, established Mikve Yisrael, an agricultural school, near Jaffa. The Alliance later opened a trade school in Jerusalem, too.

The German *Hilfsverein der Deutschen Juden,* founded in Berlin in 1901, aimed to help Jews in East Europe and in the Oriental countries. The *Hilfsverein*, known in Israel as *Ezra*, established schools with German as the prevailing language.

When the pioneers of the First and Second *Aliyot* started to come, new tongues were added to the Yiddish, Hebrew, Arabic, Ladino, English, French and German. The newcomers spoke a little Hebrew but mainly Russian, Polish, Ukrainian, Lithuanian and Rumanian. From our perspective, decades later, we can now appreciate how great was Ben Yehuda's courage and idealism.

Ben Yehuda arrived at the beginning of the First *Aliya* in 1881, with one goal: to transform the ancient Holy tongue into a living, spoken language. He introduced the Sephardic accent and he himself composed a modern Hebrew dictionary. His enthusiasm was contagious and the new *Yishuv* was seized with a burning desire to speak Hebrew. This enthusiasm produced immediate results. The ensuing dates read like a fairytale: 1880: the school in Rishon L'Zion began to teach all subjects in modern Hebrew; 1892: additional schools of this type arose throughout the country. 1903: Hebrew teachers at a conference in Zichron Yaacov founded a teachers union, which, among other things, was to issue textbooks for the schools. 1904: the *Vaad Halashon* (Language Commission) was founded, as the authority for Hebrew terms in agriculture and in industry. From then on, things went smoothly. 1905: the Hebrew *gymnasium* was founded in Jaffa. The same year, a national-religious *cheder, Tachkimoni,* was also founded.

When the building of Tel Aviv was started in 1907, the cornerstone of the Herzlia *gymnasium* was laid, and the next year the Jaffa *gymnasium* was opened there. Boris Schatz opened his famous art school, *Bezalel,* in Jerusalem in 1906, while a Hebrew *gymnasium* was opened there in 1908.

Much earlier, the first World Zionist Congress in Basle, Switzerland, dreamed a dream: to create a Hebrew University in Jerusalem. In 1901, the fifth Congress adopted the resolution proposed by Dr. Chaim Weizmann to implement this dream. In 1913, the *Hovevei Zion* of Odessa purchased some land on Mount Scopus, and in 1918, a year before my arrival, the cornerstone of the Hebrew University was laid there.

Hebrew gained ground. In 1907 the *Hapoel Hatzair* newspaper appeared as a bi-weekly, and later as a weekly. It rapidly became the publication in which the most important Hebrew writers and poets appeared and their talents were nurtured. The journal also became a tribune in which the diverse political, social, national and ideological views of the labor movement were aired. In 1908, Ben Yehuda launched a daily Hebrew paper, *Hazvi*, and in 1910, *Poale Zion* began its own Hebrew publication, *Ha'ahdut*.

At the eighth World Zionist Congress, Nahum Sokolow proposed that Hebrew become the official language of the Zionist movement. In a brilliant Hebrew speech, Dr. Sokolow stressed that the language was a unifying force and urged that all Zionist bodies promote the use of Hebrew and Hebrew culture. The entire session was conducted in Hebrew.

When the Haifa Technion was opened, there was a mass demonstration and rebellion which has had few parallels in the history of educational institutions. The idea of establishing the technological college came from the *Hilfsverein*. Much of the money came from two Jewish philanthropists: Wissotsky, in Moscow, who gave a hundred thousand rubles, and Jacob Schiff, the American, who matched it with a hundred thousand dollars. The remainder was contributed by Jews all over the world. The *Hilfsverein* began construction of the campus on Mount Carmel. Since they had a majority on the committee, they decided that the language of instruction would be German. They could not understand how physics and chemistry could be taught in any other language, especially the language of Moses! This triggered a sharp protest. Three Zionist committee members—Ahad Ha'am, Dr. Shmaryahu Levin and Dr. Yehiel Tschlenov—resigned in protest and began a struggle under the leadership of Dr. Levin. The *Yishuv* responded with outrage; thousands of teachers and pupils left the *Hilfsverein* schools and held classes outdoors. Simultaneously, Hebraists sat down to create a new Hebrew vocabulary for the courses. The *Hilfsverein* surrendered. The

146

theories of Pythagoras, Pascal and Newton were taught in the tongue of Moses and the Prophets.

In 1919, when we arrived in the country, the process of replacing the polyglot languages of the young immigrants with the reborn national tongue was well underway. By 1922, the British mandatory power recognized Hebrew as one of the three offical languages of Palestine, along with English and Arabic.

SICKNESS STRIKES

I HAVE MENTIONED THE INCIDENT IN GAN SHMUEL, WHEN I cleared up the filthy water of the pool to make it fit for bathing after our working hours. That project drained me of my energy. Some time later I felt ill. I was extremely tired, my neck was stiff and I could barely breathe. Walking was painful. I went to the Sephardi doctor in Hadera, who examined me and said that I had a bad chill, the beginning of malária, and he ordered me to apply cupping glasses. There were no cupping glasses (*bankes*) in Gan Shmuel and they had to be brought from Karkur, not far away. I asked my comrades in Gan Shmuel to send someone for the glasses but they said I had to go myself because no one could be spared from work.

My condition notwithstanding, I rode a horse to Karkur. It was a hard trip, but I came back in one piece. I lay down and a comrade started to arrange the *bankes* on my back. When he placed the first heated glass on my shoulder I yelled to him to stop at once, because I could not take it. I felt seriously ill; the doctor did not make the right diagnosis.

I asked the treasurer of the *kvutza* to give me fare to Tel Aviv to see a doctor, but he said there wasn't enough money and that I was making too much fuss about my condition: it must be a case of malaria, just like so many others had and it would soon pass. I turned to the unofficial leader of the *kvutza*, Comrade Koller, and told him that I was dangerously ill and must have money to get to Tel Aviv immediately or else I would die. Koller told the treasurer to give me a pound. I started on foot to the railway station near Gan Shmuel. I dragged myself along and midway I heard the whistle of the approaching train. I knew that I had to catch it, for there was only one train daily. With my last ounce of strength I got there in the nick of time, and clambered aboard as the train started to move forward. I stretched out on the floor of the car, breathless. Other passengers came to my rescue, pouring water on my head and giving me a drink from their bottles, which passengers used to carry in those days. A couple of men sat by me and gradually I recovered.

The train consisted of five coaches, and I was in the middle one. Near Lod, the last two cars were suddenly uncoupled and the locomotive with the three forward cars continued, but instead of speeding up they rolled along more slowly. I was frightened to see that the two loose cars were gaining on us and would crash into my coach. I jumped from the train and fell into a ditch. Fortunately, nothing happened to me. Some of the passengers who stayed in the car were slightly injured. As the train halted, the passengers who kept an eye on me jumped off and began to seek me out. They found me unscathed in the ditch. After the two cars were connected, we continued to Lod where we got off and waited for a second train to take us to Tel Aviv.

In the waiting room, a group of young people encircled a man in a Legionnaires uniform, who was addressing them. I came closer and found out that he was Berl Katznelson, of whom I had heard so much but had never seen. The crowd was very respectful and listened like a cluster of *Hassidim* to their *rebbe*.

Berl Katznelson was a leader of the labor movement in Eretz Israel. He had come to the country in 1909, at the age of twenty-two. Born in Bobroisk, in the Minsk district, he was the son of Moshe, a merchant who was an observant Jew and scholar active in Jewish educational affairs.

149

Berl received a traditional upbringing. He was devoted to Bible study and studied from the sources at a very young age. In his father's house there was a rich library in which Berl immersed himself, drinking up the wisdom of the books and periodicals. He also consumed many Russian books.

When Moshe Katznelson died, Berl's mother was left with a house full of children. Berl went to work in the Bobroisk library for *Yeshiva* students. Later he became a teacher in the school of the *Hevra Mafitzei Haskala* and also taught in a nearby village. When about fourteen or fifteen, Berl became interested in Jewish politics, and attended meetings of *Poale Zion,* the *Sejmists* and the *Narodnaia Volya.* Gradually, he began to participate in the debates. He lectured on Jewish history, sociology and economics. Astutely, he transformed abstract ideas into concrete theories, especially when he waged battle with *Bundist* preachers.

For a time he was attracted to the S.S. (Socialist Zionists) who did not believe that Jews had a future among the gentiles in Russia. Berl became familiar with all the thought currents but joined no particular party.

In 1909, he took a freighter to Jaffa and proceeded to Petach Tikva to work in the citrus groves. He spent his free time in Ein Ganim where he struck up a close friendship with A. D. Gordon. He did not agree with all of Gordon's ideas and they had many heated discussions.

From Petach Tikva, Berl went to Ben Shemen and Hadera, then to Sedjera in Galilee, and ultimately to Kinneret. There he began to organize mutual aid institutions among the workers. In Kinneret, he organized a strike against the farm manager who made light of the workers and was hard on them. As a result of the strike, the farm was given over to the workers who began to work it on their own.

In 1916, Berl, together with S. Lavi and M. Ruthberg, created *Hamashbir,* which collected the produce of the *kvutzot* and labor farms in Galilee and sold it directly to the consumers in Judea at a minimal price.

150

When the British entered Palestine during the war, Berl helped organize the 40th Battalion of the Jewish Legion and enlisted himself.

The Jewish workers were divided into two main parties, *Hapoel Hatzair* and *Poale Zion*, but many preferred to be non-partisan and belonged to neither. Berl was among the latter. His non-partisanship stemmed from his belief that all workers should belong to one unified party, especially when the war would end and a mass of new *Halutzim* would start to come. While yet in the Legion, Berl discussed the subject of a united labor movement with David Ben Gurion, Yitzhak Ben Zvi and others. In February 1919, a conference of the agricultural workers organization was held in Petach Tikva. Some fifty-eight delegates participated—19 *Poale Zion*, 11 *Hapoel Hatzair*, 28 non-partisan. There were also nineteen representatives of the Jewish Legion.

Hapoel Hatzair averred that the time was not yet ripe for full unification and the dissolution of the parties, but they were for the full unification of the economic and mutual-aid activities. After a lengthy, passionate discussion, the great majority cast a vote for total unification, whereupon *Hapoel Hatzair* delegates left the hall. The remaining majority decided to create *Ahdut Ha'avoda*, adding that the new organization would be a branch of the World *Poale Zion* movement as well as of the World Zionist Organization. It would also participate in the Socialist International.

Berl Katznelson, the leading spirit of *Ahdut Ha'avoda*, became editor of its weekly *Kuntress,* and later a founder of many economic and cultural institutions. When Histadrut was founded, he edited its daily, *Davar.* Berl Katznelson was no doubt one of Israeli labor's greatest teachers and spiritual leaders, combining a lofty spirit and a talent for practical work.

Now, as I saw Berl Katznelson in the Lod waiting room, surrounded by his admirers, I could discern the loyalty and profound respect written on their faces.

We reached Tel Aviv in the afternoon. I went straight to the *Kupat Holim* of *Hapoel Hatzair* as I had been instructed to in Gan Shmuel. Jacob Efter, the secretary, was seated in the office. He sent me to Dr. Leon Puchovsky and asked me to report back after the doctor's examination.

Dr. Puchovsky asked me a peculiar question: did I have a wound on my foot? I removed my shoe and saw nothing. He then asked if I had any wounds on my hand. At first I saw nothing, but suddenly noticed a small infection on the fourth finger of my right hand. Dr. Puchovsky examined it and started to shout in Russian: "You young whelps are irresponsible! You should have come right away when you got sick. I want you to know that you are very sick and have to get to a hospital at once. I'll give you a letter to the hospital director, Dr. Chissin. Go to his home since he has left the hospital for the day."

He banged the table, crying out, "If for any reason you don't get to the hospital today, I give you here a prescription for a medicine that you must take right away. You must also see to it that someone is with you all the time until you get into the hospital. You must not be alone because you could drop in the street."

In the letter to Dr. Chaim Chissin, he wrote that he suspected I had *tetanus* and should get into a hospital at once. I went to Dr. Chissin's home and knocked on the door. He opened a small window through which I passed the letter. He read it, took a look, gave it back to me and shouted: "Come to the hospital tomorrow morning!"

Exhausted, I returned to Efter at *Kupat Holim* and told him what had happened. I gave him the letter, which was written in Russian, and after reading it he said that I was critically ill. He found me a room for the night and assigned a comrade to sleep in it with me. He also got the medicine prescribed by Dr. Puchovsky.

Next day I was accompanied to the Jaffa hospital by my roommate. Quite a crowd was already there and I took my place in line. Dr. Chissin arrived, gave a nervous look at the patients, and called out: "Where is the fellow who came to my house last night?" When I answered, he summoned a nurse and told her to put me in bed immediately. When the nurse began to undress me, I lifted my arms in order to remove my undershirt, and began to choke. She grabbed a pair of scissors and cut off the shirt and placed me on the bed. I was seized with spasms, my body stiffened and my mouth closed tightly. This was the beginning of the tetanus attack. The doctor came immediately and ordered them to give me bromide, and put pillows under my head. I began to breathe more freely but continued to get spasms, my mouth clamped tight, and it was hard to swallow the medicine.

Dr. Chissin called Dr. Puchovsky and the two of them decided to prescribe baths in lukewarm water to relax the body and reduce the spasms. How to put me in the tub was a problem. When the nurse and an orderly wanted to lift me, I went into a spasm and had to be put back on the bed. When I calmed down a bit, they tried again. I signalled that they should handle me slowly. When they got me to the tub, there was a new problem: my body was stiff and the tub was too short. Carefully they placed my bottom half into the tub and when I became more flexible they bent me so that I was totally submerged. After a while I relaxed and felt much better, but the spasms recurred occasionally.

My nurse, Shoshanna Auerbach, treated me most loyally, like a mother. Every free moment she came to ask how I felt. In the middle of the night she peeked into the room to check up. This gave me much encouragement and I was grateful to her.

My condition was so serious that it was necessary for someone to be at my side constantly. My friends volunteered to come to the hospital to be with me, taking turns at caring for me. One of them was a *chaver* who had only recently come to Palestine from Poland and spoke no Hebrew. He was sitting with me when for some reason my head moved off the

153

pillow and I began to choke. I called out: "Avir, ruach," but he did not understand me. In desperation he yelled back: "Speak Polish!" I then realized that he did not understand Hebrew, so I told him in Polish to raise my head and put it back on the pillow.

I could scarcely move. My body and limbs were stiff and I could only wiggle my fingers. I would grasp the sides of the bed until the spasms would pass. I must confess that despite the constant pain I never fell into a mood of resignation. I had a strong will to live and did everything possible to help myself.

While asleep at night, when my body was most relaxed, I would open my mouth a trifle and stick out my tongue. But when I had a spasm, I would bite the tip of my tongue; when they gave me the bromide medicine my tongue burned. This was my plight for about two weeks.

Suddenly I developed fever. My doctors became uneasy and called for a consultation among six physicians. I remember only three names: Chissin, Puchovsky and a woman named Gutman, the wife of the famous Hebrew writer, S. Ben Zion. There was also a doctor from Hadassah, another one from the hospital and a German from the German Sharona Coldny, who was not allowed to practice as he belonged to "the enemy" camp. However, he was a great specialist and the others took the risk to include him in the consultation. He made his own diagnosis and then they began to discuss my illness in another room, so I could not hear. But the door was open and I strained to listen. One said that I had only an hour to live, a second two hours. And so on. But I did not get excited and murmured through my teeth, "I will live, I will live."

Two hours later it seemed that the crisis was over. I began to feel better. The spasms subsided. Gradually it became easier to open my mouth and my entire body began to move. I stayed in the hospital for a while longer to recoup my strength. I was surprised one day when David Remez came to visit me. He remembered me from Gan Shmuel. Because of his call at the hospital, I became a "very important person." Look! David Remez himself has paid a sick call on me.

The son of Jacob Fichman, the noted writer, was in the same hospital. One day we both read the newspaper *Doar Hayom*, published by Ben Yehuda's son, Ittamar Ben Avi. In one of the articles there was the expression *ee efshi*. The young Fichman said that it was a mistake, it should have been *ee efshar*. But I explained to him that *ee efshi* was correct, meaning "I don't want." He began to laugh at me, since he was a student at the Herzlia *gymnasium* and I was merely a greenhorn from the farm and shouldn't argue with him. I suggested that when his father comes to visit him, we would ask about it. Jacob Fichman did come, and when he heard the argument he laughed and told his son, "You are a *gymnasist* but he knows his Hebrew better."

I grew better from day to day. My appetite improved and my strength returned. I strolled around the hospital to exercise my muscles. I saw the other patients. One newcomer was down with a high fever. Flies crawled on his face and he made no effort to chase them away. The doctor said to me, "This patient is in great danger; yet in comparison with what you went through his is a light case. But you fought and had a powerful wish to get well while he has resigned. He doesn't even lift a hand to chase away flies."

Many comrades came to visit. One brought a telegram from my father which had come to the *Hapoel Hatzair* office. Cabling from London, he wanted to know what had happened to me and if I needed some money or anything else. Later I found out through a comrade who visited me, that someone had written to his mother in Poland that I was seriously ill. It seems that his mother showed the letter to my mother. When my father went from Canada to London in order to bring the family from Poland to Montreal, mother insisted that he find out what had happened to me. My father went to the Zionist Organization on Great Russell Street in

London and inquired how he could contact me. By chance, Joseph Sprinzak was there and he gave my father the address of *Hapoel Harzair* in Tel Aviv. That was how he could wire me.

I wanted to notify my parents about my condition and asked Dr. Chissin for permission to leave the hospital. He granted it, but said something that I have never forgotten: "You should know as far as medicine is concerned you were a dead man. If you were religious I would say that it was a miracle from heaven, that God helped you, but as I know that you are not'so religious all I can say is that your healthy heart and extraordinary will to live saved you. Be healthy and strong." He gave me a prescription and told me that I could not return to work for a while. I needed a few weeks for recuperation.

I went straight to *Kupat Holim* and Efter reserved a place for me at Pension Barash, where the distinguished writer Jacob Rabinowitz was also staying. Before leaving comrade Efter, I asked him to get some money together so I could telegraph my father. This began a chain of events which throws light on the conditions which then prevailed in the country. Efter said that *Kupat Holim* had little money, and it had already spent quite a bit on me. He couldn't do anything more and I would have to settle on writing a letter instead of sending a telegram.

I knew my father was worried and I had to answer his telegram at once. I went to the bank, *Halvaa V'Hisachon*, where I showed my father's telegram and asked for a one-pound loan, promising to repay it as soon as my father sent me money. The bank answered that it did not make any loans without the guarantee of a businessman. I was discouraged by this and asked for the bank head, Bezalel Jaffe. They gave me his address and I went to his home at once.

I knocked on the door and a young woman answered. I told her I wished to see Mr. Jaffe. Seeing my halting gait and emaciated face, she tried to dispose of me by saying he wasn't in. In a desperate voice I insisted that I had to see him. Evidently, Jaffe heard the bickering and he appeared and invited me in. Jaffe was a handsome man with a beautiful beard. He was dressed in a silk robe. Politely he asked me what I wanted and I told him my story, including the reaction of the bank to my request for a one-pound loan.

"Then what do you want of me," he asked.

I took out the note and asked him to sign as my guarantor, which he did with a smile. "I like your *chutzpa*," he said. "I hope you will repay the loan when you get the money from your father."

I grasped the signed note and went happily to the bank. Upon getting the pound sterling, I went to the post office and shot off a telegram to my father. A few days later, thirty pounds arrived from London. I hastened to the bank to repay the loan and then to Jaffe to show him the receipt. He thanked me and invited me to visit him again—as a guest.

Now a word about Dr. Chaim Chissin. He was among the first *Biluim*, having come to the country in the 1880s. He wrote a book of memoirs of that period, *Diary of a Bilu*. After working as a farmhand in the settlements, he went to finish his study of medicine in Switzerland. He returned to practice his profession in Russia. In 1905 he came back to settle in Eretz Israel, rising to great prominence in the *Yishuv*. A founder of Tel Aviv, he was one of its first inhabitants.

Dr. Chissin was a familiar personality in the neighborhood, as he rode through it on a white donkey. Frequently, children would tease the donkey which would bray, and they enjoyed the comic caper. Dr. Chissin's efforts to chase the kids away were of no avail.

Pension Barash was a home for learned men. Writers would vacation there for weeks at a time. I enjoyed listening to their erudite conversations. From time to time I visited the *Hapoel Hatzair* office and met leading party members. One day, a symposium on "Nationalization of the Land" was held at the Herzlia *gymnasium,* in which the participants were Joseph Aaronowitz, editor of *Hapoel Hatzair,* Dr. Chaim Bogrushov, of the Herzlia *gymnasium* and Notte Goldberg of *Ahdut ha Avoda.* Aaronowitz opened the proceedings with the thesis that the land should belong to the Jewish people rather than be in private hands because the latter could sell it to foreigners, or speculate with it, thus driving up prices. He maintained that if the land were nationalized it would be possible to adhere to the principle of Jewish labor. Dr. Bogrushov held that private investors should not be discouraged from buying land, to which Aaronowitz replied: "Take Petach Tikva, one of the important older settlements. In fact it is not a Jewish but an Arab colony because the Arabs work on the soil and are the watchmen, and I am afraid that some fine day these same Arabs will attack the settlement and make a pogrom."

The warnings of Aaronowitz unfortunately were to become realities. In May 1921, two years later, Arabs from thirty-six villages attacked Petach Tikva. Among the attackers were Arabs who had worked there for years; their wives and children came with sacks to take home the loot. A day earlier the Arabs took home the horses of their employers and the cattle that they had pastured. They attacked Petach Tikva from all sides—they knew every point of entry very well. The sons of the Jewish settlers, together with the Jewish laborers, put up a heroic defense and the Arabs fled, leaving scores of dead and wounded. The Jews lost four dead and fourteen injured.

After this, the Arabs did not return to work in Petach Tikva for a long time, and the landowners employed only Jewish workers. Eventually the Arabs filtered back to work for their former Jewish employers again.

THE "RUSSLAN"

ON DECEMBER 19, 1919, THE THIRD DAY OF HANNUKAH, A boat brought 620 passengers from Odessa to Jaffa. Representatives of *Hapoel Hatzair* met the newcomers and helped them get their bearings. Zvi Lieberman was in charge of the arrangements and as I was in Tel Aviv at the time, he took me along to meet the *Russlan*. It was an unforgettable experiance.

It rained heavily. The Mediterranean was a stormy mass of water. Because of the huge waves, the boat could not come close to shore. Rocks jutted out of the raging waters and it was dangerous for any ship to enter the port. The *Russlan* dropped anchor out at sea.

Lieberman hired an Arab who was to take us out to the *Russlan* in his boat. We sat in the small boat, while the Arab craftily steered it in the heavy downpour. Every few minutes a large wave lifted the boat like a child's toy; suddenly a threatening rock appeared in front of us and the Arab began to wail: "Allah! Allah!" Somehow we got to the *Russlan* safely and climbed up a rope ladder which the sailors lowered to us.

On deck we were surrounded by the passengers, among whom were Dr. Joseph Klausner, Dr. Moshe Glikson, Dr. Abraham Katznelson, Lipman Levinson, Avraham Revusky and Yehuda Lev-Tov. There was also the Hebrew poet, Ra-

159

chel Bluvstein, who was returning from Russia where she had spent the war years.

Since it was impossible to approach the docks of Jaffa, the captain decided to steam toward Haifa. Meanwhile the storm died down and the ship turned back to Jaffa where all debarked. In 'the port, hundreds of people were waiting to tender a hearty reception to the new arrivals. It was a joy to see such a large number of Russian Jews coming at.one time. They were hugged and kissed; even strangers were embraced. Everyone hoped that this was only the beginning of a large *Aliya*, that thousands more would soon follow.

A public reception was organized for the distinguished personalities who had come on the *Russlan*. Dr. Klausner and Dr. Glikson spoke. Revusky, a leader of the *Poale Zion* was also supposed to speak. He announced that while he knew Hebrew he would speak in Yiddish. Dr. Klausner and others accused him of suppressing Hebrew culture when he was the Ukrainian Minister of Jewish Affairs in the beginning of 1919. A tumult broke out. Members of the *Gdud Meginei Hasafan*, defenders of the Hebrew language, lifted their chairs and were ready to throw them. Revusky did not make his speech.

This incident astounded me and was entirely unexpected. After the reception I gave it much thought. I spoke Hebrew and Yiddish fluently. Like many others, I understood why it was essential to introduce Hebrew as the spoken tongue of the country and what a role Hebrew could play in uniting the diverse Jewish tribes who had come from so many different countries with so many different languages and cultures. Nonetheless, not to allow a member of *Poale Zion* to speak in Yiddish, and to bar him by force, made a negative impression on me.

I returned to Pension Barash and stayed a few more weeks. Meanwhile, I received a letter from my father. He found out how seriously ill I had really been and wrote that I should come "home" forthwith. That meant to go to Canada, where the whole family now resided, parents, brothers and sister. I answered that I felt better and wanted to remain in Eretz Israel.

A week or two later the doctors decreed that I should no longer go back to Gan Shmuel where there was a lot of malaria. I must settle down in a healthier climate.

Kupat Holim of *Hapoel Hatzair* arranged for me to go to Kvutzat Hulda in Judea.

HULDA, TRUMPELDOR AND TEL HAI

HULDA WAS ONE OF THE TWO AREAS WHERE THE JEWISH
National Fund had purchased land for the planting of the
Herzl Forest. The other place was Ben Shemen. The two
farms were established by the Zionist Organization and became training centers for planting trees. A two-story house
was built at Hulda for the workers. It was far from a luxuri-
ous abode. The bottom story was half sunk in the ground and
insects would crawl through the windows while the air in our
sleeping quarters was damp.

When I went from Tel Aviv to Hulda after my illness, I
was given a friendly welcome and accepted at once as a
member of the *kvutza*. There were-twenty-seven members,
twenty-two men and five women. Four of them had just arrived from Poland, including three from my Lodz group:
Simcha Grosbard, Jacob Skosovski and Yehuda Rubin. The
farm consisted of 850 dunam of field crops, 750 dunam
of olives, 115 dunam of almonds and fruits, and 115 dunam
covered with various trees.

Among the members were leaders of *Hapoel Hatzair*:
Aaron Ben-Barak, Chaim Izus and David Ben-Yishai who
were later to become founders of the first *moshav* Nahalal.
In addition I must mention Yitzhak Caspi, who was sent
later to Europe to help organize the *Aliya*, but he became
sick and died at an early age. Among the *kvutza* leaders were
also Chaim Shurer, later editor of the Histadrut daily *Davar*;
Nahum Lichtman and Haya Barash.

162

In the mornings we went out with our hoes to soften the earth around the trees and to water the small ditches. The more experienced comrades tended the trees and pruned the branches. When the fruit ripened we picked it. I made every effort to adjust to the *kvutza*, working hard in spite of my weakened condition. I went out each morning to the orchards with my hoe, to dig around the trees. As in many of the settlements, there was a water shortage. Between our Hulda and Arabic Hulda there was a well which served both settlements. We went to the well with a wagon and cans to fetch water. One morning I went with another comrade, a native of Ekron, to the well and saw an Arab girl with a jug on her head. She was young and pretty and I began to flirt with her. Suddenly, out of nowhere, an Arab youth sprang toward me flashing a knife. Instantly my comrade dashed toward the Arab and yelled that I was a *Muscobi*, a Russian, and he had better not touch me since I meant no harm—my flirtation was purely an attempt to be friendly. My would-be attacker withdrew and I escaped unscathed. It turned out that the young girl was the sheikh's daughter and the young Arab was her intended groom. The epithet *Muscobi* was highly respected by the Arabs and its invocation averted who knows what consequences.

We spent the evenings talking about farm problems and matters that faced the working community. Discussions were held almost daily. A lot was said about the duties of the workers on the eve of the great wave of *Aliya* that was expected. The newly developed idea of *moshav ovdim* was also a constant topic. After a day's work, the debates were quite refreshing.

I remember a triple wedding of three sisters that took place in Hulda. It was a beautiful affair, with guests coming from the surrounding villages. The dancing and carousing lasted all night.

The existing *kvutzot* served as training centers for new im-

163

migrants. Some of the arrivals on the *Russlan* started their careers at Hulda and then left to work at nearby Kfar Uriah. In 1912 Jews bought the land and house at Kfar Uriah. A group of laborers occupied the courtyard, among them Aaron David Gordon. The place was isolated, far from Jewish settlements, and it lacked water. During the first World War workers abandoned the place and after the war, the owners came to build homes for themselves and moved in.

In the rainy season we could not work outdoors, so we read. *Hapoel Hatzair* began publishing a monthly magazine, *Maabarot* (Transitions) edited by Jacob Fichman. It was a literary journal that also dealt with public affairs. It carried poems, stories, literary criticism and essays, original and translated. Contributors were from inside the country and abroad. The magazine introduced me to the works of many good authors. From time to time I travelled in the vicinity, visiting Ekron, Rehovot, Rishon L'Zion and Gedera.

Many prominent guests came to Hulda. One of them was Joseph Trumpeldor, the living legend himself. I looked at him with awe and respect and recalled the highlights of his colorful career. Trumpeldor's father was a soldier under Czar Nicholas I, and served twenty-five years in the Russian army. He gave his son Joseph a broad secular education and sent him to a Russian *gymnasium*. When the Russo-Japanese war erupted in 1903, Joseph joined the army and was posted to Port Arthur. He lost an arm in the conflict and spent a year in a Japanese prison. Upon his return to Russia he resumed his studies at the *gymnasium*, and then enrolled in the university, where he was introduced to Zionism.

In October 1912 Trumpeldor went to Eretz Israel and worked in Degania. When the Turks exiled Russian Jews, he went to Alexandria. With Zev Jabotinsky he sought to create a Jewish military unit as part of the British army. The British did not accept this idea but proposed a Jewish transport outfit to support the British troops in the Dardanelles. Jabotinsky was against it, but Trumpeldor accepted the British prop-

164

osition and the Zion Mule Corps was created. Jews who had been driven out of Palestine by the Turks to Egypt volunteered for the Corps, which chalked up a heroic record. Under heavy fire, the Corps supplied material and food to the front line troops. After the British withdrawal from the ill-fated Dardanelles venture, Trumpeldor returned to Alexandria.

When the Kerensky Revolution swept Russia in 1917, Trumpeldor returned there in pursuit of a dream. He envisioned a legion of young Russian Jews who would march through the Balkans to Palestine. However, pogroms flared up in the Ukraine and Trumpeldor decided to stay and participate in the Jewish self-defense. He traversed hundreds of miles of Russian territory, organizing armed self-defense units. He set about organizing *Hechalutz* (The Pioneer) to prepare for early *Aliya* to Eretz Israel, going from town to town, village to village. He wrote a pamphlet setting forth the principles of *Hechalutz* and organized groups that would go on a training farm. Meanwhile the Bolsheviks took over. Full of energy and conviction, Trumpeldor surmounted the Bolshevik chaos and antagonism. *Hechalutz* grew in numbers.

Trumpeldor returned to Eretz Israel to survey the facilities for absorbing the pioneers and planned to return shortly to Russia to organize the flow of *Aliya*. But that was not to be.

Arriving in Eretz Israel in November 1919 and finding the country dislocated because of the war, and intolerable feuding between the two labor organizations, he tried to hammer out an agreement between *Hapoel Hatzair* and *Ahdut Ha'-Avoda*. He met with leaders of both camps. On December 10, Trumpeldor wrote a letter, published in the *Hapoel Hatzair* and the *Kuntress*, calling on the workers for united action:

Russian Jewry is being driven out, and the Jewish masses stand with packs on their backs, waiting for the doors of

165

Eretz Israel to open. Behind them lurk destruction and pogroms.

And what lurks on the other side of the doors? What is happening inside Eretz Israel? The Zionist institutions suffer from a shortage of funds, there is a shortage of initiative and there is unemployment. And what about the working masses? When I left Eretz Israel at the start of the war in 1914 there were two parties: *Hapoel Hatzair* and *Poale Zion*. They waged an ideological contest, but on the economic front they found a common answer. There was a joint agricultural organization and a general *Kupat Holim*. Now this is not the case. *Hapoel Hatzair* has its own "office" and *Achdut Ha'Avoda* has its own "labor bureau." There are two *Kupat Holims*, two agricultural workers organizations and even two railway workers unions.

I have many longtime friends in both parties. We have worked together, fevered together, faced danger together here in the country and in Gallipoli. Together we have loved this land without reservations. I love and respect all my comrades in both camps. And who dare not respect the veterans who stood constantly at their posts? They also loved each other and respected each other. But now one can not speak to the other without gritting one's teeth. I have listened to the complaints of both sides; I have tried to penetrate the reasons and I have tried mightily to suspend my own views in order to be objective. In the end I came to the conclusion that there is a basis for cooperative action and it is possible to create cooperative institutions.

Eight months ago such an attempt was made but it did not succeed. What should we do now? After a series of private talks that I had last month with some comrades of both parties, it is my opinion that an agreement can be found on the following basis:

The parties will continue to exist in the future. The workers who do not exploit others, shall choose delegates for a joint council on the basis of proportional representation. Other parties and groups may set forth their lists. The council will be non-partisan and will establish joint institu-

166

tions and authorities: a) a labor bureau, b) an information bureau, c) a *Kupat Holim*, d) immigrant hostels, e) restaurants, f) evening courses, g) loan societies. The council will assist in the formation of trade unions. The council also has the right to decide upon and execute activities which have the agreement of the delegates of all parties. In cases where there is no unanimous agreement, any party can undertake it as its own activity. Parallel with the council there should be created non-partisan trade unions which can later be united into a non-partisan organization.

Of course, the existing trade unions must be converted into non-partisan organizations and must work in conjunction with the council.

The central committees of both parties must come to agreement about this. If necessary a conference of the elected representatives on the council should be convened.

I repeat: The Jewish people are facing great events. In a month or two or perhaps the coming years the fate of the Jews in Eretz Israel will be determined. But the Zionist leaders are not prepared for great deeds. They have no plan. On the other hand, there is a danger of more pogroms which will have no match. The Russian Jews are on the threshold of Eretz Israel and beg: "Let us in!"

Extraordinary efforts must be made to create a united labor movement. Every one who will come will be rescued from death or from a life of persecution. Exert yourself to emerge from the partisan framework and help solve the cardinal problems! Help those on the threshold of Eretz Israel so that they may enter. Save them!

This was the call of Joseph Trumpeldor. The response was instantaneous. Two weeks later, on January 6, *Achdut Ha'-Avoda* sent a letter to *Hapoel Hatzair* signed by S. Yavnieli, advising that "in reply to the letter of Joseph Trumpeldor about creating joint institutions elected by the Israeli workers, we hereby announce that we accept the proposal and we are prepared to realize it. We ask you to express your attitude toward this proposition. If you answer positively we are pre-

pared to meet at once to work out the methods of coopera-
tion."

Next day *Hapoel Hatzair* replied:

We have your letter of January 6th. You know, of
course, that Trumpeldor's proposal was published after he
had negotiated with our comrades. If not all the details, at
least the principal ones that he mentioned were suggested
by our representatives. He attempted to make an end to the
sharp civil strife among the workers of Eretz Israel for the
past year.

We are pleased with your communication and accept the
proposal. But we wonder why the *Kuntress* and your letter
to us are silent on one of the main principles, the creation
of non-partisan trade unions. The existence of partisan
unions is not acceptable in the world at large and especially
in our life. The experience of division had verified this: the
entry of certain trade unions into *Achdut Ha'Avoda* led to
the creation of parallel organizations in the same trade
(e.g. agriculture, printing). Many workers who were against
the establishment of parallel unions in their trades belong
to no organization. Parallel unions create friction, conflict
and arguments in the day-to-day work.

The creation of joint general organizations while the
daily trade union activities are divided and generating hostility, will certainly not improve matters.

We wish to clarify the details of our proposal which in
the main is incorporated in Trumpeldor's proposal. . . .

Here the *Hapoel Hatzair* set forth its views that the unions
should not have any links with political parties; that existing
unions get out of the parties to which they belong (leaving
such membership up to the individual members); a conference of agricultural workers should be called to set up a non-
partisan organization; a central information bureau, sick fund
and other institutions would be set up under a joint council
elected by all the workers in the country; and so on.

Letters were exchanged over a period of time. Theoretical

168

debates were held. A year later, thanks to Trumpeldor's initiative, a conference was convened in Haifa, and Histadrut, the general federation of Jewish workers in Eretz Israel, was founded. That was in December 1920.

When Trumpeldor was visiting Hulda and I had the privilege of meeting him in person, the unification debate was in full swing. Unfortunately, Trumpeldor did not live to attend the founding conference that he espoused. News had come that Arabs were attacking Jewish settlements in Galilee. Blood was shed in the northern settlements of Metulla, Hamara, Kfar Giladi and Tel Hai. Trumpeldor went up to Galilee, pulled by his heart to head the struggle against the Arab assaults. On Sunday, March 1, 1920, he died in defense of Tel Hai. When the conference of workers that he inspired was convened the following December, he was not present to see the realization of his dream, the dramatic response to his call for labor unity in the land of Israel.

The manner in which Trumpeldor and his comrades fell at Tel Hai will remain a glorious chapter in Zionist history. The Bedouins had revolted against the French, who occupied Syria and northern Palestine. They also attacked Christian settlements loyal to the French, killing the residents, burning their houses and pillaging their villages. At first they did not bother the Jews but they did attack solitary passersby on the roads and take their possessions.

In mid-December 1919, an armed band of Bedouins attacked Tel Hai. The comrades inside the *kvutza* resisted heroically and the Arabs withdrew. One of the defenders, Shaposhnik, was wounded in the fight.

The territory under British control was quiet. The British region included Yessud Hamaaleh, Safed, Mishmar Hayarden and Rosh Pinna. There one could transport livestock and goods and not be afraid. But a bit further up, in the French zone, there stretched a Death Valley; all the way to Metullah there was a constant unrest and a sense of insecurity. Thievery was the order of the day.

There were about twenty-five people at Tel Hai and eighteen at Kfar Giladi. They had few weapons and little food. The settlers issued a call for reinforcements, and armed comrades came from Upper and Lower Galilee, from Kinneret, Degania, Bet Gan, Merhavia, Givat Hamoreh, Ayelet Hashachar and Machnayim.

Trumpeldor arrived on January 1, 1920, with some comrades. On the way to Hamara he was attacked by Arabs, who undressed him stark naked and took off with his clothes. However, they did not get his revolver. He cast it into the weeds. Covering himself with sackcloth, he made his way to Tel Hai and began to organize the defense.

The members of Tel Hai and Kfar Giladi worked in the fields every day, accompanied by armed *Shomrim*. Once they heard an exchange of shots. It was a fight between the Bedouins and a small French patrol. The French retreated to Metullah and the Bedouins followed them. On the way they ravaged Christian settlements. In one attack on Tel Hai, on the 17th day of Shvat, one comrade was slain, Aaron Sher, a volunteer from Kinneret. This was the second sacrifice.

Friday, February 28, thirty-five people came from Ayelet Hashachar, among them Sarah Chizik. The next day it was a quiet Sabbath. Sunday morning, when Trumpeldor was having breakfast with the comrades at Kfar Giladi, shooting was heard from the direction of Tel Hai. Immediately, Trumpeldor and several comrades dashed to the scene and saw that the courtyard was surrounded by armed Bedouins. Together with his eight comrades, Trumpeldor entered the house and took up defensive positions. A witness later recalled how the leader of the Bedouins, who had fought against the French, Kamil Effendi, accompanied by four Arab officers armed with revolvers and grenades came to Tel Hai and accused the Jews of hiding Frenchmen. They demanded access to the house so that they could see whether or not there were French troops there. Since this was not the first time that such demands had been made, they were granted entry. The officers searched the rooms but one of them separated from the others and signalled to the Arabs outside. From all sides throngs of Arabs headed toward Tel Hai.

Meanwhile, Kamil and the other officers went with Trumpeldor into the house where they inspected all the rooms on the first floor, then they went up to the second floor where Dvora Drachler, Sarah Chizik, Benjamin Munter, Wolf Sharf and Chaim Kanevsky were stationed. Suddenly, Dvora shouted: "Trumpeldor, they have taken my revolver!" Trumpeldor commanded that they shoot into the air. He ran to the gate to hold back the Arab mob but on the way he was wounded.

Trumpeldor commanded that they shoot at Kamil and the officers. He went out into the courtyard again. This time he was seriously wounded in the stomach. Jacob Toker, who tried to traverse the yard to help Trumpeldor, was hit by five bullets. A member of the Jewish Legion stole his way to the spot where Kamil Effendi was standing with his officers and began shooting at them. At the same time he grasped Trumpeldor and dragged him into the house. The wound was fatal. Knowing this, Trumpeldor handed over the command to Pinhas Schneurson. He directed his comrades on how to bandage him, saying, "These are my last moments. You must all stand at your posts until the last minute and fight for the honor of the Jewish people."

Heavy gunfire flared up. Kamil and his cohorts went to the roof to seek an escape route, but they were targeted by the defenders, who also shot from the windows and from the barn at the mob outside, killing and wounding many Arabs. The attackers shot into the windows, and the defenders replied with grenades. Suddenly there was an explosion in one of the second floor rooms. Kamil turned to one of the comrades asking to be let out so that he could order the Arabs to halt the attack, but they did not trust him and didn't give him clearance. Later Kamil renewed his request. Considering the tough situation, he was allowed to get out. Other comrades, who did not know of this deal, began shooting at him

171

when he tried to get off the roof. Finally, he was allowed to go through the gate. The shooting ended for a half hour during which time the Arabs retrieved their dead and wounded.

The comrades brought in the body of Toker. When they began to climb a ladder to the second floor, the Arabs opened fire again. The Bedouins came closer, yelling wildly: "Don't be afraid of them! Go after them!" But they did not attack. They only asked that one of the comrades come out to talk to them but this was a ruse. When a comrade exposed a hand he was wounded by a grenade. When the Arabs realized that their strategy would not work they began to hurl flaming torches. Two Jewish grenades came back at them and the Arabs fled. It was quiet in Tel Hai.

When the comrades broke through a wall and crawled into one of the upper rooms they found a horrible scene. Covered with pillows and blankets, hidden behind tables and chairs were the bodies of Benjamin Munter, Sarah Chizik, Dvora Drachler and Wolf Sharf. They heard groaning under a blanket and discovered the wounded Kanevsky.

Dusk arrived. Severely wounded, Trumpeldor ordered three comrades to try to reach Kfar Giladi to fetch a doctor and six more men. The three, armed with revolvers and rifles set out, crawling on their bellies, until they reached Kfar Giladi. They found fifteen comrades who were ready to come along with the doctor.

Trumpeldor and Kanevsky were wrapped in blankets so they could be transported to Kfar Giladi. Trumpeldor died on the way. His last words were: "It is good to die for our country!"

A wagon was sent from Kfar Giladi to bring the bodies of the dead from Tel Hai. From a grove Arabs opened fire on the group. Some comrades went ahead with the wagon while others stayed back to return the fire. After loading up the most valuable property of Tel Hai on a wagon, they set fire to the buildings. Two o'clock in the morning, when it was pitch dark, they buried the dead. The remaining hours were spent fortifying Kfar Giladi. Water was brought in, bags were filled with sand, and bread was baked. They were ready for the siege.

Shooting started at dawn. Orders were issued not to waste ammunition. The attackers tried all day to penetrate the house but they failed. During the evening, the defenders analyzed the situation. They knew that the Bedouins would storm Kfar Giladi with all their might. It was decided that twenty-seven persons would leave and twenty-six would remain. They would pull out only if the Arabs attacked with cannon.

A massive array of Arabs began to stream toward Kfar Giladi, on foot and on horseback. The comrades decided to make a stand, but when the boom of a cannon was heard and the hordes of Arabs began to move headlong toward them, they eluded the eyes of the Arabs and escaped across the far side of the hill. The Arabs milled around for five hours, throwing grenades into the house before trying to enter. The withdrawing comrades reached the Arab village of Taibe where they were given a friendly reception. Meanwhile, comrades arrived from Metulla. When the *Bek* asked where the other comrades were and heard that this was the whole group of defenders, he could not believe it—so few facing such a huge force, a force from which even the French had fled.

At night the comrades went to Ayelet Hashachar. Scores of workers from Judea, Samaria and Lower Galilee were on the way to Tel Hai and Kfar Giladi with wagonloads of food, medicine and weapons. Unhappily, they came too late. They heard the sad news that Tel Hai and Kfar Giladi were destroyed and that after the heroic death of Trumpeldor, the survivors had to leave the two *kvutzot*.

The entire *Yishuv* was angered by the behavior of the Representative Committee to which the Tel Hai defenders had sent a special emissary asking for help. The Provisional Committee sat complacently, and after some discussion suggested that the settlements be evacuated because they did not have the strength to defend them. They did not even send food, let alone weapons. The Representative Committee did not appreciate the historic importance of a strong defense as it was understood by the settlers in Upper Galilee. They did not understand that positions should not be abandoned after they had been built up with so much hard work, blood and sweat, without a formidable defense. The comrades of the settlements did not heed the advice of the committee and paid for their decision with their lives.

When the Peace Conference held in San Remo on April 24, 1920, awarded two mandates, Palestine to the British and Syria to the French, the boundaries were drawn so that Upper Galilee, including Tel Hai and Kfar Giladi, which had been so heroically defended, were on the side of the British mandate, within the territory of the future State of Israel.

SELF-GOVERNMENT IN THE YISHUV

WHEN THE TURKISH REGIME WAS OUSTED FROM PALESTINE at the end of the first World War, it was expected that the British occupying power would open a new, bright chapter in the life of the *Yishuv*. When I arrived, the aftermath of the Turkish repression was still omnipresent. But the new British regime did not seem to offer much relief. It was to be a long road until Jewish aspirations and rights were to be firmly established.

Early in 1918, when the British army had taken Judea, the British government sent a Zionist Commission to Palestine to study the situation and prepare plans for the future, in the spirit of the Balfour Declaration. Among the objectives of the Commission were:

(1) Establishment of connections between the *Yishuv* and the British authorities.
(2) Coordination of relief work and repatriation of exiles and refugees.
(3) Reestablishment and development of rural Jewish settlements.
(4) Help organizations and institutions disrupted by the war.
(5) Create friendly relations between the Jewish and Arab communities.

The Commission represented Jews of the chief Allied countries: England, France and Italy (the Russian representatives were unable to leave Russia). The English members were Professor Chaim Weizmann, Joseph Cowen, Dr. David Eder, Leon Simon, Israel Sieff and Harry Sacher. The French contingent consisted of Professor Sylvan Levy (an anti-Zionist) who was president of the Alliance Israelite Universelle, and James Rothschild. The Italian was Commandant Levi Bianci. Weizmann headed the Commission, which arrived in Alexandria on Passover eve, 1918. Shortly thereafter it went to Palestine.

The Commission met with the British military administration, which was hostile to Zionism. The *Yishuv* was exhausted, disorganized with impoverished settlements and a shortage of essential goods. The old *Yishuv*, the *Haluka* Jews who were mostly elderly people, lived in their own special world, remote from modern realities.

The war had cut off their sources of income, charity from abroad. They used to send Meshulachim (emissaries) to Jewish communities around the world, especially to Europe and America, to collect money for religious Jews. During the war this income was cut off, but they received support from the rescue fund of the American Zionists. Their current income was from the Joint Distribution Committee. which had provided the money for distribution among the *Haluka* recipients through the Zionist Commission.

Aside from relief work, the Commission saw to the improvement of sanitary conditions in the country.

When British forces occupied Southern Palestine at the end of 1917, the question of electing a representative body of the *Yishuv* arose.

On January 2, 1918, representatives of political parties, educational and economic institutions in Judea met in Jaffa to consider ways of organizing a representative assembly. Some proposed a constitutional assembly as a prelude to forming a parliament. After long debate, it was agreed that such a step was premature, but it was decided to convoke an *Assefat Hanivcharim*, an elected assembly, that would encompass all sections of the *Yishuv*; it would establish central institutions in charge of education, social welfare, health and other public concerns, as well as represent the *Yishuv* vis-a-vis the British administration.

An interim committee, *Vaad Hazmani*, was elected to supervise elections for the assembly. On January 11, 1918, the second preparatory conference was held. Half a year later, when Galilee was liberated by the British, a third conference was held.

The Provisional Committee tried to consolidate all segments of the population—the old and new *Yishuv*, the religious and the secular, the numerous parties, the diverse institutions, to prepare for the Representative Council. Each Jew would be entitled to vote, regardless of class or sex. However, the Orthodox fought against the inclusion of women. The Jerusalem rabbinate and the *Mizrachi* used every tactic, fair and foul, to block the elections on the issue of women's suffrage. The Provisional Committee went on with its task, determined to hold elections in October 1919. At the last minute, the Zionist leadership ordered a temporary halt to the election activities.

The Zionists stressed that they would not waive any of the rules proposed by the Provisional Committee, especially the voting rights of women, but they reluctantly decided to ask for the postponement of the elections until a more propitious time. At the moment, there were too many external problems before the San Remo Conference and internal dissension would merely give ammunition to the opposition. The Provisional Committee bowed, and the elections were deferred until April 19, 1920. Then they were conducted with full participation of the entire *Yishuv*, including the women. Fifteen slates were submitted.

Of the 28,765 eligible voters, seventy-seven percent cast ballots, and two hundred fifty-eight members were elected to the *Assefat Hanivcharim*. Labor lists got a majority, followed by the Sephardim. At the same time the larger cities of Jerusalem, Haifa and Tel Aviv elected city councils, and local councils were chosen by the smaller communities. At the initiative of the British authorities, two rabbinates were elected: *Sephardic* and *Ashkenazic*.

The first session of the *Assefat Hanivcharim* was held in Jerusalem on October 7, 1920. The *Vaad Leumi*—national council—was elected as the autonomous national leadership of the Jews in Eretz Israel.

Assefat Hanivcharim was recognized by the British mandatory power as the official representative of the Jews, with the right to levy taxes for educational and health budgets. The first chairman of the *Vaad Leumi* was the noted Hebrew writer and educator David Yellin. *Assefat Hanivcharim* met annually for twenty-eight years, until the founding of the State of Israel in 1948. All these years, Yitzhak Ben Zvi headed the *Vaad Leumi*.

POGROM IN JERUSALEM

WHEN THE WAR ENDED AND THE BRITISH SUCCEEDED THE Turks, the Jews believed that the new occupying power would usher in a bright chapter in the history of the *Yishuv*. When I came to the country I could still find the bruises inflicted by the Ottomans, but the British administration did not seem to be much more friendly to the Jews. British hostility was evident everywhere. The new rulers put roadblocks in the way of *Aliya*. They forbade the singing of *Hatikva* in public.

In the summer of 1919, the military command in Palestine prepared a list of over 150 soldiers of the 40th Battalion of the Jewish Legion then posted in Rafah, to be sent to guard prisoners of war outside Eretz Israel. The Jewish Legionnaires refused to obey the order, arguing that they had enlisted in order to serve inside the country and not outside its borders. The British threatened the Legionnaires with a court-martial. They sent the British Jewish chaplain to persuade the Legionnaires to obey orders and not give the Jews a bad name: that they had rebelled in a most non-military fashion. The Legionnaires stood their ground. Finally, the High Command in Egypt intervened and the order was rescinded.

Meanwhile, the Arabs exploited the anti-Jewish bias of

the British, and launched their own disorders. An anti-Jewish campaign had been going on in Jerusalem for some time. Agitators in the Arab press and at Arab religious convocations called for attacks on the Jews. The British watched but did nothing.

The *Yishuv* demanded that the government arrest the agitators, whose identities were well known, but the British did not react. On the contrary, with British connivance, Arab demonstrations against Zionism were held. These manifestations were not merely "anti-Zionist," but blatantly anti-Jewish, inciting to attacks against Jews. Single incidents occurred at the Western Wall and other locations in Jerusalem.

The Jerusalem Jewish Council protested to the British authorities but to no avail. There was absolutely no response. The Arabic newspaper, *Southern Syria*, published a manifesto to the Arabs: "If our protests are not heard, let us protest with deeds. Instead of the pen let us take to the sword; instead of ink, let blood flow!" The Council complained to the governor of Jerusalem about this outrageous manifesto that was being circulated in thousands of copies, but it did not help. The paper was not suspended.

On Sunday, April 4, 1920, during Passover some five hundred to six hundred Arabs flew banners and demonstrated in Jerusalem. They stopped at an Arab club near the Jaffa Gate. The newspaper editor made an inflammatory address: "If we do not use force against the Zionists and the Jews, we shall never get rid of them!" A sheikh, echoing this line of thought, railed: "Whoever has a stick should go and root out the Jews. Only thus will we be rid of them once and for all!"

The demonstrators looted the shop of a Jewish watchmaker. A British airman who happened by tried to protect the shop but was stabbed to death. The mob then assaulted other Jewish businesses on the block and any Jew they could pounce upon. Arab mounted police pretended that they were breaking up the riot but they hit only Jews. The turmoil lasted a half hour, and not a single British soldier was visible.

The Arabs swarmed to the Old City and entered the gate. Meanwhile, some twelve hundred Jews hurried to the scene, young and old, armed with sticks and tools. They rushed toward the Old City to defend the Jewish Quarter. When they reached Jaffa Gate, the British locked it and threatened the Jews with machine guns. Under no circumstances would they let the Jews enter. The narrow street leading to *Bikur Holim* was also surrounded by British troops.

Arab hotheads inside the Old City began to harass the Jews. Hadassah ambulances brought out the first victims. The Arabs continued their pogrom undisturbed. After an hour and a half, the outside Jews were allowed into the Old City. One witness reported: "When I entered, I saw a picture that we Jews used to see in Russia. Feathers and bedding, battered utensils, broken furniture and torn goods were scattered over the street. Bleeding Jews were everywhere. As a result of this shocking incident, Jews lost faith in the British 'peacekeepers.' From all sides came the call: 'Take away your police. We'll defend ourselves.' "

Many Legionnaires had come to celebrate Passover in Jerusalem. The British went about arresting the Legionnaires in order to prevent their helping the Jewish inhabitants. At one point there was a clash between a British patrol and a Jewish self-defense unit. With the assistance of Arabs, the British disarmed the Jews. Another Jewish outfit was arrested and held for several hours.

The British slapped a curfew on the area, keeping everybody indoors after six o'clock in the evening. They assured the Jews that attacks would be halted; this was only an empty promise.

Next morning at eight o'clock, there was another Arab religious demonstration in Jerusalem. The government did not disturb the demonstrators who were escorted by Arab police as they marched toward the Mosque of Omar. A Jewish witness later recounted: "A group of us Jewish youth got into the Old City and saw the first Jewish victim fall near the Amdursky Hotel. The Arabs divided into gangs, some going onto the roofs from which they shot down and threw stones at the Jews. Others assaulted the victims on the streets, hitting and robbing them. A Jewish policeman named Radowilski was seriously wounded and taken to hospital."

Radowilski later related that when he had gone into the Old City with other policemen, two of his Arab colleagues led him into an alley where they signalled to an armed Arab band; one of the Arabs took away his revolver while others stabbed him.

When the pogroms broke out, four leaders of the *Vaad Hatzirim*—Menachem Ussishkin, David Yellin, Mordecai Eliash and Rabbi Mordechai Nurock— went to the military commander of the area and submitted the following memorandum:

a) The Arab police demonstrated that they could not maintain order and prevent pogroms. There are reports that Arab police participated actively in the pogroms. The Jews are not safe as long as the protection continues to be in the hands of the Arab police. We therefore demand that the protection of the inhabitants be assumed by the British police.

b) Further demonstrations and meetings with incendiary talks addressed to the masses can trigger more pogroms. We therefore demand that Arab demonstrations, parades and meetings be forbidden.

c) We fear the repetition of 'the Nebi-Mussa parades. We therefore ask that the government prohibit the demonstrators from passing through the city or come near to it.

d) The morning riots caused tens of injuries, among them several in a critical condition (we do not as yet know how many are dead). Businesses were ruined, much Jewish property was stolen. The mob cursed at and reviled the Jews. These riots were organized by Arab agitators and Arab clubs. We demand that these clubs be shut down and the agitators be arrested.

We also demand that an investigation commission be appointed, in which Jews shall be included. Its task should be to determine the facts and the amount of damage caused to Jews. Those responsible for the riots must face a military court and the thieves must pay for the damage.

But the riots in Jerusalem did not cease. It was obvious that the British stood aside but leaned toward the Arabs. Weapons of all Jewish Legionnaires in Jerusalem were confiscated. The authorities manipulated it so that the Jewish police would not be near the riot sites. Jews were not allowed to enter the Old City but Arabs came and went freely.

After the pogroms on Saturday and Sunday, the British declared a state of emergency and gave the responsibility of protecting the city to the military. Jews were subject to a six o'clock curfew but the Arab murderers and pillagers roamed around the streets and executed their attacks against Jewish homes unhindered.

It was relatively quiet on Monday, but Tuesday morning the riots resumed and twenty Jews were wounded during the day. That day, Zev Jabotinsky organized nineteen demobilized Legionnaires and led them to the gate of the Old City to defend the Jews. Immediately, British patrols arrested Jabotinsky and his comrades. The news spread throughout the Jewish community, and Jews were greatly aroused by it.

Rabbi Yitzhak Kook, the chief rabbi of Jerusalem, called upon the Jews who were in the synagogues to ignore the fact that it was the Passover holiday and sign a petition to the authorities to demand Jabotinsky's release. The same day, the Representative Committee sent a telegram to the Foreign Ministry in London:

On April 4 there began a pogrom on the Jews of Jerusalem; eight were killed and over two hundred injured; two women were raped. Much Jewish property was destroyed.

Preparations for the pogrom were made over a long period of time. Single attacks on Jews occurred frequently. Despite many Jewish demands and warnings, the government did not use its military against the instigators of the pogroms but against the Jews who tried to defend themselves and their brethren. Arab police participated in the pogroms. The pogrom makers boasted openly that the government was on their side.

We demand that an investigatory commission be sent to study the behavior of the administration toward the Jews during this period and especially since the outbreak and duration of the pogroms.

The telegram was signed by the Provisional Committee of the Jews of Eretz Israel.

The Israeli press accused the military administration of conducting a one-sided policy against the Jews. *Kuntress*, official organ of the *Ahdut Ha'Avoda*, editorialized:

We accuse the British occupation power of being responsible for the pogroms that have broken out in Jerusalem. . . . The English administration has given to the Arab police the task of maintaining order but the police itself participated in the pogroms. . . . When Jewish representatives informed the government that Arab police were involved in the pogroms and demanded to exclude them, they were not listened to. The Arab police remained in the Old City, in the Jewish streets, and the pogrom endured several days.

The government did not take the necessary measures to investigate the acts of murder and robbery. The majority of the murderers and robbers go about frank and free over the streets of Jerusalem with the guarantee that nothing will happen to them.

On April 12, *Hapoel Hatzair* printed an editorial entitled, "Blood of Jerusalem":

Jewish blood has been spilled in the streets of Jerusalem, innocent blood which can not be forgotten and which can not be paid for. That which has happened in Jerusalem these three days will never be forgotten. The mark of Cain will remain on the brows of the government officials who had the opportunity to protect the victims. They did not do it and did not allow the Jews to defend themselves.

This was not a blind outbreak but a calculated political intrigue organized by sharp minds. The pogroms began with demonstrations against Zionism, with the permission of the government, and ended with the slaughter of Jews in Jerusalem.

The entire Jewish people will claim compensation for this bloodshed. The human conscience will arise against the barbarous deeds of the implementers of the Balfour Declaration in Eretz Israel. The sentence is one: punish the murderers, punish the guilty British officials. We demand the opening of the doors for Jewish immigration.

On April 19, Jabotinsky and his comrades were court-martialed. Jabotinsky was sentenced to fifteen years in prison at hard labor while his comrades got three years each. At the same time that Jabotinsky received such a harsh sentence, the Arab agitators went scot free. Others were sentenced, not as inciters to murder but only for making speeches without a permit. It was clear that General Bolls and his cohorts were out to sabotage the Balfour Declaration and the idea of a Jewish homeland.

On the next Sabbath Jabotinsky and his comrades were taken to the Acre prison. The Jews of Jerusalem were horrified at the stiff sentence and because the arrestees were jailed on the Sabbath. It was decided to go out on a protest strike the next day. The Jews did not open their shops on Sunday and all the factories and institutions were closed. No Jewish wagons moved on the streets. Groceries and bakeries were shut. Schools were not in session. Men and women gathered in the Sephardic synagogues to recite psalms. In other synagogues, the shofar was blown as a symbol of sorrow. At 10:30 a.m. the government ordered all businesses to open and sent police to the proprietors, but the businesses were shut tight until noon when the strike ended.

We in Hulda, like the members of all other *kvutzot*, kept tabs on the scandalous behavior of the British authorities. We were angry at the British, as were Jews the world over, for tolerating pogroms in the land of Israel.

Deputies in the British parliament made inquiries about the pogroms and the incarceration of Jabotinsky. The government replies were evasive. Colonel John Patterson, the commander of the Zion Mule Corps and a Zionist sympathizer, speaking in London, declared, "My heart told me in advance what would happen. I knew that among the British administrators in Eretz Israel there were people who hated the Balfour Declaration and wanted to appease the Arabs. . . . Jabotinsky was tried because they hated him, because he was an intellectual and because he had opposed the administration's anti-Jewish policies."

The Jewish mood changed with the April 24 decision of the San Remo peace conference. The peace treaty gave the Palestine Mandate to Great Britain and the Balfour Declaration was incorporated into the Mandate agreement. Henceforth, the Jews hoped, Britain would introduce a civilian administration, and its policies would accord with the Balfour Declaration—the undertaking of the British to facilitate the establishment of the Jewish national home in Palestine.

Sir Herbert Samuel was appointed first High Commissioner of Palestine. He proclaimed an amnesty for all political prisoners but Jabotinsky refused to accept this. He did not want a pardon but insisted on a complete nullification of his sentence. In time, the British relented and rescinded the verdict.

Optimism prevailed upon the arrival of Sir Herbert. But for me it was a time for a new chapter in my own life.

I AM FORCED TO LEAVE THE HOMELAND

AFTER A PERIOD OF RECUPERATION, I RETURNED TO HULDA. During my incapacitation, a great transformation occurred in the life of my family. My father had brought my mother, brothers and sister to Canada. When he discovered that I was seriously ill, he began to bombard me with letters to join them in Montreal. I wrote back that I was determined to remain in Eretz Israel.

But my condition did not improve. Periodically I fell sick, prey to a multitude of diseases, and had to go to the hospital in Jerusalem. Going to Jerusalem was good for body and soul. I took advantage of these medical trips to see the city as well. The first thing I did was to go to the greatest magnet of all, the Western Wall. Seeking my way to the Wall, I met a young man dressed in the traditional *Hassidic* fur-trimmed hat and a long coat. In Hebrew, I asked him the way to the Wall and he replied in Yiddish. I asked him if he knew Hebrew. Smiling, he said that he knew the language very well, but it was the Holy Tongue, not to be spoken in the street or in "vulgar" places.

Passing through the narrow streets, I reached the Wall and touched its massive stones. I began to quiver although I was not particularly religious, and recited a prayer. For a long time I stood there, unable to tear myself away.

On another occasion I visited the *Bezalel* art school, founded by Boris Schatz. It was the first art academy in Eretz Israel. My guide was a cousin of mine, also from Lodz, named Rubin. Boris Schatz was a Lithuanian Jew and sculptor. He proposed to Theodor Herzl that an art institute be established in Eretz Israel. Herzl liked the idea and submitted it to the seventh World Zionist Congress in 1905, which sanctioned the plan. A year later, Schatz settled in Jerusalem, where he opened the school named after the Biblical artist who supervised construction of the Tabernacle and designed the clothing of the ancient priests. The school attracted many students from the very beginning, some coming from abroad. *Bezalel*'s purpose was not only to perpetuate the symbolism of the Bible in the spirit of Jewish legends and folklore but to create a modern Jewish style.

My cousin Rubin was a teacher in the school. Others were: Abel Fahn, Ephraim Lilien, Nahum Guterman and Ephraim Fald. Rubin escorted me around the studios and workshops where I got an idea of how much these pioneers of Jewish art had accomplished, parallel to the accomplishments on the soil of my comrades in the *kvutzot*.

My father did not stop writing me. He also wrote to my friends from Lodz who were in Hulda. He begged them to influence me to go to Montreal. He wrote that he had discussed my case with doctors and they all agreed that my illness weakened me so much that I could not recuperate in a hot climate. My comrades showed me his letters but I told them that I was convinced that the doctors were wrong and that I would soon recover completely and I would remain in Eretz Israel.

Stubbornly, I continued to work at Hulda, but I grew weaker as time passed. I had to rest more frequently and could not keep up with the others. Just as I was stubborn in my decision to remain, my father insisted that I leave and join the family. He wrote not only to me but to the *kvutza* leaders, pleading that they send me "home."

188

Then something happened that tipped the scales. I developed a high fever and had to go to a Jerusalem hospital. The doctors confirmed that I had contracted typhus. After a few days in the hospital I had an unexpected visitor, Chaim Shurer. He told me that the *kvutza*, after a consultation with doctors, had decided that I must leave the country and go to a land with a cooler climate. Otherwise I would never regain my health. I answered that the comrades were wrong, as I definitely felt better. I argued that the present illness was a passing one that could have hit anyone, and declared that I had come to Eretz Israel to realize a childhood dream and that I would stay. Shurer answered that it was clear to them that I would be unable to work for a long time. Would I want to be a parasite in the group? I wept. I had to accept the verdict of the *kvutza*. After leaving the hospital I returned to Hulda, defeated and resigned.

The comrades insisted that I stop working in order to regain some strength but I categorically refused. Until the day I actually left, I would be like all the others.

I went about in a melancholy mood. My friends from Lodz, especially Skosovski, comforted me, saying: "We are your comrades who grew up with you and dreamed together about Eretz Israel and together we realized our dream by coming here. We know how strong your determination was in Lodz and on the way through Italy. You never doubted or despaired. Now, you've had bad luck. It is not your fault. Take fate as it is."

I could no longer stand up against the will of my comrades and the pleas of my parents. With a heavy heart and many tears in my eyes, I wrote to my family that I would come. Quickly, I received a letter from my father with fifty pounds for travel expenses to London. He gave me the address of a London friend with whom I could stay. He also wrote that he was sending me, at his friend's place, a boat ticket from Southampton to Montreal and a letter to the Canadian High Commissioner in London to give me a visa to

Canada with the least possible complications, as I was a son of a Canadian citizen, and a minor.

During my last days in Hulda I thought about my fate. I reviewed in my mind the adventurous journey with my comrades from Lodz, over so many roads until we reached Eretz Israel. We came as the first harbingers of the Third *Aliya*. I thought a great deal, often bitterly, about the fact that we succeeded in getting to Eretz Israel by our own efforts; we ourselves had to break through the barriers and received no help from the official Zionist leadership. On the contrary, they frequently hindered us. During the several months we spent in Italy, absolutely nothing was done by the World Zionist leadership on our behalf, and when I say this, I do not mean financial help but only to ease our way. They had no ties with us and even did not answer our communication.

The groups that came to Italy during the months we were there, the comrades from Lodz, Bendin, Sosnowitz, Radom and also individuals from Galicia, received assistance in the various Italian cities only from local leaders. In Trieste there were Dr. Dlugatch, Rabbi Zoller and Attorney Karp. In Rome there was Dr. Moshe Beilinson, Dr. Jacob Bluvstein and Rabbi Dr. Dante Lattes. In Naples there was Dr. Wigdorchek.

These and only these encouraged us, helped make contact with the Italian government as well as with local governmental people. They even sought to get for us refugee funds, free train rides and transportation on the ship to Alexandria. They helped us, not the central Zionist institutions.

Later we found out that at the first session of the Zionist Actions Committee after the war, in February 1919, to which we sent a telegram, our question was not dealt with at all. The Zionist leadership was not interested in our going to Eretz Israel. With cold logic they argued that first there must be a systematic organization of the immigration, and the ground must be prepared for the absorption of newcomers.

190

In June 1919, a second session of the Actions Committee was held in London. Justice Louis D. Brandeis headed an American Zionist delegation. Brandeis participated in the meeting only two days as he was enroute to make his first visit to Eretz Israel. Accompanied by Jacob de Haas, Dr. Harry Friedenwald and Robert Szold, he spent only two weeks in Eretz Israel and in such a short period could not truly become acquainted with the problems of the country. He visited a few settlements and made a disparaging remark about them that sorely grieved the settlers. He departed with the opinion that if the basic sanitation work was not done, immigration should not be encouraged. On September 9, 1919, he reported to the national executive committee of the American Zionist Organization about his personal evaluation of conditions in Eretz Israel.

Brandeis foretold that not only masses of Jews from eastern and southern Europe would come to the country but also Jews from Oriental lands. According to his view, immigration should be restricted as it would depend on how many people the land could accommodate. He declared categorically that unless a sanitation program was implemented, until malaria was uprooted, *Aliya* should be discouraged. He expected the British mandatory power to drain the swamps and pave the roads.

Meanwhile, immigration went on at a limited pace. Only small groups made their way to Eretz Israel on their own initiative. An editorial in *Hapoel Hatzair*, dated February 13, 1920, bears witness. Under the caption, *Hevlei Aliya*, Birth-pangs of Immigration, the editorial noted:

A group of the new *Olim* who arrived these days from Galicia, Poland, and Czechoslovakia has reported that it was not enough that various governments created difficulties in the path of *Aliya*; the Zionist organization does the same. . . . In the Palestine Office in Vienna, the young immigrant is met coldly; in a truly bureaucratic manner the

191

request of the *Halutzim* for confirmation of their documents so that they may obtain visas from the British to enter the country, is denied.

"We don't need you in Eretz Israel! There is no work for you. Go back home!" These are the usual "friendly" words with which the official representatives of the Zionist organization greet the tens and hundreds of *Halutzim* in the Austrian capital and other cities. These *Halutzim* have been waiting for months and years at various transit centers on the road to Eretz Israel.

We don't know whether the Palestine Bureau acts on instructions from headquarters, or each "ruler" does it on his own. The fact is that the central committee of *Hapoel Hatzair* gets dozens of letters from *Halutz* groups who urgently press for help to overcome these obstacles which rob them of the possibility of reaching their goal.

The question of emigration is urgent and requires an immediate answer. Promises are worthless as long as the gates of Eretz Israel are closed to Jewish immigrants. If we can have differences of opinion with those who demand that the gates be thrown wide open so that we can rescue tens of thousands of Jews from Russia and the Ukraine from annihilation, and with those who demand an organized *Aliya*, there can be no difference of opinion on the immediate need to open the gates for the principal builders of Zionism, for the *Halutzic* forces without whom we can not visualize the upbuilding of the land.

. . . It is entirely untrue that there is no work in Eretz Israel—it is clear that the work which must and can be done now, even under present circumstances, is not being done and will not be done as long as the Zionist organization is ruled by the thought that we must await the arrival of fantastic sums of money, and as long as it will think that immigration can be achieved only by Jews who have the means to arrange for their own absorption.

The editorial goes on to state that for a year or two previously there had been no jobs in the country, at least less than there were now, yet hundreds of young people came and were supplied with work, regardless of whether the work was desirable or not. They settled down, and so would others in the future. People will come and jobs will be created! But if they do not come, the editorial warned, wild grass and thorns will grow in the desolate fields of Zion.

The editorial ended on the note that "nothing will come of itself. If we speak earnestly of preparing the land, of preparing ourselves for mass immigration, then it must be clear in advance that people and working hands are required. These people and these working hands will not come from among the rich Jews and the owners of estates, who expect to sit in the Diaspora while a safe and peaceful haven is prepared for them in Eretz Israel. The builders will come from the ranks of the young volunteers, the hosts of *Halutzim* whose entire fortune is only a bit of national enthusiasm and a national will—for such as these there is always a need! Let them come on *Aliya*!"

I read these words and felt bitterness in each and every syllable. My comrades and I had experienced the incomprehensible and often destructive action of the official Zionist institutions. Whatever their merits in other phases of Zionist endeavor, in this field they were flagrantly derelict.

EPILOGUE

WHEN IT BECAME CLEAR THAT I MUST LEAVE THE COUNTRY, I fell into a depression. Such a disappointment! All my youth I dreamed of going to Eretz Israel, to participate in the up-building of the Jewish national home. I left my family, my closest friends, and ventured forth with a group of comrades on an unknown, bumpy road. Months on end we roamed in alien cities, living in strange hotels and railway stations. After countless hardships we at last reached the Promised Land.

Eretz Israel—then, as the Third *Aliya* dawned—mostly was a wilderness with craggy hills, desolate fields, malarial swamps. Among my comrades I felt no strangeness. Together we would reclaim this wilderness for our people. Every tree that we planted and nourished in the sun-baked soil brought us closer to our goal, closer to the rebirth of the Jewish homeland.

Now, hard work was beyond my powers. Weariness and exhaustion replaced the dynamic energies of my youth. But I was conscious that I was participating in the realization of our dream. Even the severe illness that struck me down did not dampen my enthusiasm for a moment, nor, more impor-tant, did it diminish my will to live, to get well, to regain my ability to proceed with thousands of other *Halutzim* to do the job of rebuilding ourselves, our land and our nation.

And now, this crushing disappointment.

What induced me most to make this sorrowful decision to leave the country was not the parental letters but the arguments of my comrades, who told me that I would never be able to work as a peer among them, that I would be dependent. Engraved in my mind are the words of Chaim Shurer: "Do you wish to be a parasite in the *kvutza*?"

I knew they were right, that I must depart. From the moment I recognized the justice of their position and I decided to go away, I spent the evenings in bed. I couldn't stop thinking of the past. . .about the days in the scout movement in Zgierz. . .of our fantasies inspired by such Hebrew novels as *Ahavat Zion* and *Ashmat Shomron*. I thought of the times we squatted around the campfires and sang *Seu Ziona Ness VaDegel*—bear the flag and banner to Zion—and *El Yivneh Hagalil*—God will build Galilee—and numerous other melodies. How we sang and wove dreams and told tales of the heroes of *Hashomer*!

Pictures floated back into my mind—how we paraded through the streets in our scout uniforms and sang on high pitch, *Ya Hai Li Li Ama Li Li*, accompanied by fife and drum, how in Lodz we diligently studied Palestinography and knew by heart all the details of a landscape, the rivers and lakes and *wadis*, the hills and valleys of our homeland.

My comrades in Hulda saw my depression. I spoke intimately with those from Lodz and sought solace among them. They tried their best. Again and again they told me it was not my fault that I had to leave; it was circumstances beyond my control. But these words of consolation helped little.

The last two days were the hardest. I went around the *kvutza* as in a fog. I ran to every corner of Hulda, saying goodbye to every tree, every bush, every flower. I stooped to bid farewell to each of these lovely friends. My comrades witnessed all this and I sensed their sympathy. On the last day as we breakfasted together, my last meal in Hulda, they reassured me that I was not leaving forever, that I would re-

195

turn, with the guarantee that when I did I would again be accepted as a member of the *kvutza*.

After breakfast I packed my few things; this brought back memories of the day I packed and left Zgierz a year and a half earlier. I was supposed to take the *diligance* to Tel Aviv and connect there for the train to Alexandria. However, something unexpected happened. A middle-aged woman and her young daughter had come to Hulda from Yessud Hamaaleh, one of the first settlements in Upper Galilee. They had heard that I was sailing for London and asked me for a favor: to escort the girl there. The daughter had recently become engaged to a Jewish Legionnaire from America. The groom was demobilized and he went home to Detroit. Before leaving, he promised to send for the girl and they would get married. Now he was in London; he had sent her papers and was waiting for her. Mother and daughter came to Hulda to seek me out as a suitable companion for the bride-to-be, who had never travelled abroad and feared to go alone on such a long journey. At the *diligance*, the girl parted from her mother while I said a final "Shalom" to my comrades. The two of us rode away to Tel Aviv.

It is hard for me to describe my mood as I left Hulda early in May 1920. Later, however, on the train to Alexandria I felt I was moving backward in time and space, reversing the direction of my entry into Eretz Israel, back through Gaza, through El Arish, to Alexandria. I sat silently at the window, observing the landscape. Near me sat the young *Sabra*, also immersed in her thoughts. I understood her uneasiness—this was her first trip abroad; she was leaving her homeland for foreign shores.

We had to wait several days in Alexandria for our boat. We took rooms in a hotel where some demobilized Legionnaires were registered, and spent our time seeing the city and dropping in on the offices of *Zeire Zion*. In the morning we took our belongings and went to the port where the boat

196

was docked. The girl went aboard, restless but full of optimism. Her fiance was waiting in London and would take her to America. In London, my ticket was waiting for me.

I sat on the deck, gazing at the distant, dark horizon, full of mixed feelings. In their letters, my parents kept repeating: "Come home! Come home!"

Did I really have a home, there in Canada? I was going to my parents, to my brothers and sister, but deep in my heart the question bothered me: How can I be going "home" when I have just left home, the home of which I had dreamed in my deepest dreams!

INDEX

Berlin, 11, 12, 112, 124
Berman, B., 19, 102
Besem, 44
Bialik, Chaim Nachman, 16, 37, 93
Bianci, Levi, 176
Block, David, 107
Blumenfeld, Eliahu, 119–20
Bluvstein, Isser Leib, 118
Bluvstein, Jacob, 72, 74, 75, 118, 122, 190
Bluvstein, Rachel, 115, 117–18, 120–21, 124, 159–60
Bogrushov, Chaim, 158
Bolls, General, 185
Bonaparte, Napoleon, 12
Bonn, 14
Brandeis, Louis D., 105, 191
Brunn, 38
Bukhara, 143
Bussel, Joseph, 98, 99, 102, 106–7

Cairo, 80, 81
California, 140
Canada, 16, 38, 114, 142, 155, 187, 197. *See also* specific cities
Caro, Joseph, 11
Caspi, Yitzhak, 162
Cathedral of St. Maria, 47
Cathedral of St. Wenceslas, 47
Central Synagogue of Genoa, 64
Ceshek, 70
Chajes, Zvi, 50–51
Cheransky, 80
Chissin, Chaim, 152–54, 156, 157
Chizik, Sarah, 170, 171–72
Chmelnitsky, Bogdan, 9
Church of St. Peter in Chains, 70
Clement VII (pope), 8
Cohen, Yusek, 74
Coldny, Sharona, 154
Colosseum (Rome), 69
Columbus, Christopher, 62
Constantinople, 9, 14, 113
Cooperman, Moshe Aharon, 73
Cowen, Joseph, 176
Cracow, 47–48, 66

Cracow University, 46
Cremieux, Adolphe, 14, 144
Crimea, 118
Czechoslovakia, 191
Czenstochowa, 46–57

Damascus, 13, 21, 106, 108, 109, 141
Daniel Deronda, 37
Dardanelles, 164
Dashevsky, Pinhas, 113
Degania, 20, 83, 98–99, 116, 121, 132, 164, 170
Detroit, 196
Diary of a Bilu, 157
Din, Baha, 109
Dlugatch, Dr., 190
Dlugatch, Mr., 56–57, 59, 61
Dombrovski, Jacob, 44
Drachler, Dvora, 171–72

Eastern Europe, 42
Eder, David, 176
Effendi, Kamil, 170–71
Effendi, Mahmed, 10
Efter, Jacob, 107
Egypt, 25, 80, 81, 139, 140, 141, 142, 143, 165, 179
Eiger, Abraham, 31–32
Eiger, Moishel, 31–32
El Arish, 83, 90, 196
Elberg, Yehuda, 29
Eliash, Mordecai, 182
Eliot, George, 37
Emek, 22
Engels, 14
England, 17, 41, 142, 176. *See also* specific cities
Eretz Israel, 8, 9, 11, 17–18, 25, 29, 38, 41, 44, 53–54, 61, 62, 64, 67, 71, 73, 74, 80, 81, 82, 89, 101, 105–6, 108, 114, 117, 118, 119, 121, 124, 125, 126, 129, 130, 140, 142–43, 149, 157, 161, 164–69, 178, 179, 185, 186–94, 196
Eshkol, Levi, 142
Eternal City, 67
Ethiopia, 143

Europe, 14, 42. *See also* specific
countries

Fahn, Abel, 188
Fald, Ephraim, 188
Father Thomas, 13
Fedon, 12
Feinberg, Avshalom, 139, 140
Feinberg, Lulik, 139
Feldman, 88
Fichman, Jacob, 155, 164
Fishman, Ada, 90, 98, 100, 125
Fishman, Yehuda Leib, 90, 125
Fiume, 59, 61
Flavius, Josephus, 79
France, 10, 11, 12, 117, 121, 129, 140,
176. *See also* specific cities
Frankel, Jacob, 11
Freund, Dr., 54, 60
Friedenwald, Harry, 191
Friedrich the Great (king of Prussia),
12
Frischman, David, 29, 37

Galicia, 191
Galilee, 19, 85, 98, 101, 105–6, 108,
115, 125, 126, 128, 129, 135, 142, 150,
169–70, 173, 174, 177, 196
Galilee, Sea of, 96, 97, 102
Gallipoli, 9, 166
Gan Shmuel, 83, 85–87, 88–89, 91, 96,
98, 103–4, 111, 127, 148–49, 152, 155,
161
Gaza, 83, 90, 196
Geiger, Abraham, 13
Genoa, 58, 62, 63–66, 67, 75, 76
Germany, 11, 12, 13, 14, 15, 41, 101,
104, 113
Giladi, D., 97
Giladi, Israel, 134
Glikson, Moshe, 159, 160
Glovinsky, Michael, 34
Glovinsky, Zippora, 33
Goldberg, Notte, 106, 158
Golomb, Baruch, 92
Gordon, Aaron David, 18, 88, 98, 100,
129, 150, 164

Gordon, Juda Leib, 15, 37, 70, 89, 90,
102
Gordon, Yael, 115
Gottlieb, Yehoshua, 43
Great Britain. *See* England
Great Synagogue of Vienna, 50
Green, David. *See* Ben-Gurion,
David
Greenbaum, Yitzhak, 43
Greenberg, Abraham, 44
Greenford, Samuel, 38
Grosbard, Simcha, 44, 162
Guinzberg, Baron, 88, 124
Guterman, Nahum, 188
Gutman, 154

Ha'am, Ahad, 146
Haas, Jacob de, 191
Hadera, 83–84, 86, 87
Haifa, 104, 109, 132, 160, 169, 178
Halberstam, Rabbi, 118
Halevy, Yehuda, 37
Hamashbir, 107
Hankin, Yehoshua, 109, 130–31, 132,
133, 134
Hanoch, Gershon, 87
Hapoel Hatzair, 88, 168
Harzfeld, Abraham, 21–22, 106–7,
108, 110
Hashomer, 134–38
Hashomer Hatzair, 42
Hebrew University, 145
Hebron, 8, 143
Hegel, 14
Herzl, Theodore, 17, 188
Hess, Moses, 14, 15
Hirsch, Samson Raphael, 13
Histadrut, 90, 108, 125, 151, 169
Hofshi, Natan, 97
Holdheim, Samuel, 13
Holland, 8
Holy Land, 84
Homel, 17
Hulda, 162, 163–64, 187, 190, 195, 196

ICA. *See* Jewish Colonization Association

201

Lipschitz, Alexander Ziskind, 32–33
Lipschitz, Mordecai Shmuel, 32
Lishansky, Joseph, 140–42
Lishansky, Sarah, 140
Lithuania, 17, 32, 132
Lod, 82, 83, 90, 149, 151
Lodz, 29, 30, 31, 32, 33, 37, 38–39,
    40, 41, 42, 43, 44, 45, 46, 50, 60, 62,
    71, 74, 80, 82, 90, 92, 94, 111, 162,
    188, 189, 190
London, 38, 155, 156, 157, 189, 196,
    197
London Zionist conference, 71–72
Ludenberg, 48
Luria, Chaim, 44, 47, 60

Magnes, Judah, 113
Maharsha, 36
Mahmud IV (sultan of Turkey), 10
Maimonides, 11
Maimonides, Moses, 10
Malkin, Sarah, 102, 115
Malta, 79
Mandelzweig, 60
Manya, 112
Mapu, Abraham, 15
Marasa, 70
Marcus, 44, 51, 52, 54, 59, 62
Marseilles, 82
Marx, Karl, 12–13, 14
Mazia, Runia, 140
Mediterranean Sea, 55, 79
Meir, Golda, 23
Meisel, Chana, 20, 119, 121, 125
Meisel, Eliahu Chaim, 40
Meisel, Hannah, 115, 117
Memories of the House of David, 37
Menachem, 47–48
Mendelssohn from Dessau, 11–12
Merhavia, 97
Messcha, 132
Mestra, 63
Metulla, 173
Michelangelo, 70
Mikveh Israel Agricultural School,
    16

Millet, Joseph, 64
Miriam, Golda, 33–34
Mishneh Torah, 10
Mohiliver, Shmuel, 85
Montefiore, Moses, 14
Montreal, 29, 38, 155, 187, 188, 189
More Nevuhim, 10
Moses, 10, 70
Mosque of Omar, 181
Munter, Benjamin, 171–72
Murenhausen, 52

Naples, 75, 76–82, 190
Nathan the Wise, 12
Nazareth, 106, 121, 132, 133, 141
Ness Ziona, 110
Netter, Charles, 144
Netzah Israel Lo Yishaker (Nili),
    139, 140
New York, 38
Nicholas I (czar of Russia), 118, 164
Nile, 79
Nili. See *Netzah Israel Lo Yishaker*
Nisanov, Yehezkel, 134
North Africa, 8
Nurock, Mordechai, 182
Nutkin, Shabtai, 96

Odessa, 44, 113, 121, 159
Odessa Lovers of Zion Committee,
    85
Oppenheimer, Franz, 97
"Our Accounting with Ourselves,"
    88
Ozerkow, 32, 33

Palestine, 15, 16, 17, 19, 20, 21, 22, 61,
    80, 90, 100, 101, 108, 109, 139, 140,
    142, 147, 151, 153, 165, 169, 174–75,
    176, 179, 186
Palestine Bureau, World Zionist Or-
    ganization, 85, 97, 107, 108, 115, 192
Palestine Commission, Zionist Ac-
    tion Committee, 101
Palestine Land Development Com-
    pany, 19, 101, 131

202

Palestine Mandate, 186
Papal Museum, 70
Paris, 112, 113
Pasha, Gamal, 20, 104, 140
Patterson, John, 186
Peace Conference, San Remo, 174
Perlman, 82
Petach Tikva, 89, 92–95, 106, 107, 115–16, 121, 125, 127, 150, 158
Plehve, Wenzel von, 112
Plinsk, Hirsch Halevi, 128
Podolia, 32
Poland, 2, 15, 17, 23, 29, 41, 42, 43, 62, 72, 80, 98, 100, 128, 129, 132, 138, 153, 155, 162, 191
Pompeii, 77
Ponto Luciano, 72, 74, 75

Port Arthur, 164
Portugal, 8
Portugali, Mendel, 134
Pro-Israelite, 71
Promised Land, 55, 194
Provisional Committee of the Jews of Eretz Israel, 177, 184
Prussian Academy of Science, 11
Puchovsky, Leon, 152–54

Quo Vadis, 69

Rabinowitz, Jacob, 156
Radom, 59, 61, 64, 190
Radowilski, 182
Rambam, 10
Rechthand-Yaffe, Shoshanno, 97
Red Sea, 8
Rehovot, 110, 131
Reichert, Zelig, 44, 83
Remez, David, 89, 90, 154–55
Representative Committee, 173–74, 183
Reuveni, David, 8
Revusky, Avraham, 159, 160
Rikovsky, D., 97
Rishon L'Zion, 139
Roman Empire, 67, 69
Romania, 17

Rome, 54, 65–66, 67–75, 76, 78, 117
Rome and Jerusalem, 14
Rosenberg, Rabbi, 36
Rosenblatt, Jesse, 43, 45
Rosenblum, Aaron, 33, 37
Rosenblum, Madam, 33
Rosenthal, Ceshek, 44, 68
Rosenwald, Julius, 140
Rothschild, Edmund de, 16, 112–13, 130–31
Rothschild, Evelina de, 144
Rothschild, James, 176
Royal Fusiliers, 142
Rubashov, Zalman, 124, 125
Rubin, Yehuda, 44, 53, 74, 162, 188
Rubinstein, Baltscha, 29, 32
Rubinstein, Eliezer, 29–30
Rubinstein, Joseph, 30–31
Rubinstein, Malkele, 30
Rubinstein, Yachtsha, 30
Rubinstein, Yossel, 31–32, 39–40
Ruppin, Arthur, 19–20, 101, 102, 131
Russia, 15, 16, 17, 18, 20, 30, 43, 72, 84, 93, 101, 104, 107, 112, 113, 117, 118, 121, 124, 157, 176, 192
Ruthberg, M., 21, 107, 150

Sacher, Harry, 176
Safed, 8, 132, 143
St. Maria Cathedral, 47
St. Peter's Church, 70
St. Wenceslas Cathedral, 47
Samaria, 85, 105–6, 131, 135, 173
Samuel, Herbert, 186
Samuel, Maurice, 122
San Remo Peace Conference, 174, 177, 186
Sapir, 65, 76
Scharf, Dr., 50–51
Schatz, Boris, 145, 188
Schiff, Jacob, 146
Schneurson, Pinhas, 171
Schnuer, Zalman, 37
Schochat, Israel, 109
Schwartz, Issachar, 29
Schwartz, Mark, 29

World Zionist Organization, 19, 151.
See also Palestine Bureau, World
Zionist Organization; Zionist Or-
ganization

Yaacov, Zichron, 16, 141
Yaffe, Eliezer, 97
Yanait, Rachel, 109–10, 111, 116–17
Yavniel, 97
Yavnieli, Shmuel, 89, 167
Yellin, David, 178, 182
Yemen, 84
Yigel, 132–33
Yitzhaki, Shlomo, 10
Yohanan of Gush Halav, 69
Young Guard, 138
Yugoslavia, 25, 51, 52, 56

Zambkovitza, 46–47
Zaslavsky, Yaacov, 97

Zecharia, 84
Zeid, Alexander, 134
Zemach, Shlomo, 19, 128–129, 130
Zerubavel, Jacob, 117
Zevi, Sabbatai, 9–10
Zgierz, 29, 30, 31, 38, 41, 42, 44, 50,
73, 80, 83, 90, 110
Zilberschatz, Abraham, 32
Zion, 7, 15, 42, 126, 193
Zionist Action Committee, 101, 190
Palestine Commission of, 101
Zionist Commission, 175–176
Zionist Conference, 74
Zionist Council of Vienna, 59
Zionist Organization, 56, 97, 130,
155, 162. *See also* World Zionist
Organization
Zion Mule Corps, 165, 186
Zoller, Rabbi, 58, 65, 190